FANTASY UNDERGROUND

How to Draw

ZOMBIES

Discover the secrets to drawing, painting, and illustrating the undead

by Mike Butkus and Merrie Destefano

Walter Foster Publishing, Inc.
3 Wrigley, Suite A
Irvine, CA 92618
www.walterfoster.com

This library edition published in 2012 by Walter Foster Publishing, Inc.
Distributed by Black Rabbit Books.
P.O. Box 3263 Mankato, Minnesota 56002

Project Manager: Elizabeth Gilbert
Designer: Shelley Baugh
Production Design: Debbie Aiken
Production Management: Lawrence Marquez and Nicole Szawlowski

Printed in Mankato, Minnesota, USA by CG Book Printers, a division of Corporate
Graphics.

First Library Edition

Library of Congress Cataloging-in-Publication Data

Butkus, Mike.
  How to draw zombies : discover the secrets to drawing, painting, and illustrating the
undead / by Mike Butkus and Merrie Destefano. -- 1st library ed.
      p. cm. -- (Fantasy underground ; falL)
    ISBN 978-1-936309-63-4 (hardcover)
  1. Zombies in art. 2. Monsters in art. 3. Drawing--Technique. I. Destefano, Merrie,
1954- II. Title. III. Title: Discover the secrets to drawing, painting, and illustrating the
undead.
  NC825.M6B88 2011
  743'.87--dc22
                                                                        2010052983

042011
17320

9 8 7 6 5 4 3 2 1

FANTASY UNDERGROUND

How to Draw

ZOMBIES

by Mike Butkus and Merrie Destefano

3

Contents

Introduction

The Zombie: to know him is to fear him.

He travels in packs, hungers for human flesh, and generally signifies the end of life as we know it. Like a scene from a 1960s horror film, his crowd of the undead appears out of nowhere. It shambles closer, revealing sunken eyes, broken teeth, and moon-pale skin that crumbles and peels away much too easily. Somehow these monsters manage to shuffle along despite missing fingers or limbs. A foot might be turned sideways or an ear might be hanging lopsided, but it doesn't matter. These creatures don't feel pain. They don't even communicate with one another. And if you think they're ambling along without direction, you're wrong.

They're on a mission; they're insatiably hungry.

And they'd love to add you to the menu.

You've just entered The Fantasy Underground, a land where nightmares emerge from the mists of imagination, a place where dark creatures are born, the ultimate playground where you'll learn how to add your own thumbprint to the ever-changing Zombie legend. Whether you're aching to learn how to draw these monsters or hoping to brush up on Zombie folklore or planning to write your own story about this popular monster, this is the right place to be. All the information, inspiration, and instruction you need is right here.

But consider yourself warned. You should probably read this book with all the lights turned on, and all the windows and doors locked. Because the zombies are loose.

And the latest rumor is they're hungry.

5

Zombie History

The Nightmare Begins

They were humans once, these beasts that populate the cinema screen, the modern novel, and the occasional nightmare. They lived, they laughed, they loved, they died—then a legendary plot twist came along: they didn't stay in the grave. They came back with a hunger and a vengeance.

They became zombies.

Risen from cemeteries and tombs, these are the walking dead.

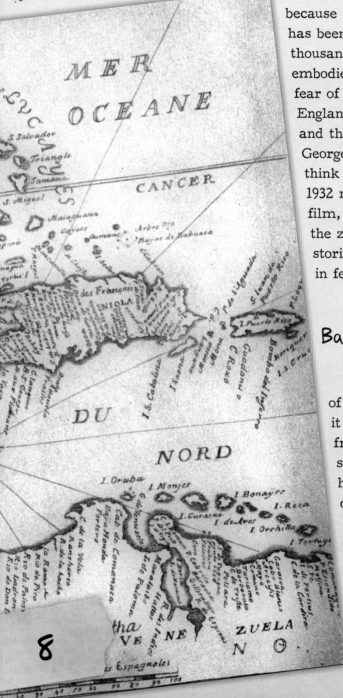

If this mythic monster keeps you awake at night, it's probably because it contains slivers of all the scariest legends. The zombie has been pieced together, a la Frankenstein's monster, over thousands of years. Swathed in tattered burial clothes, the zombie embodies our collective memories of ancestral worship and our fear of death. It has walked through the fog-shrouded history of England, Germany, Romania, Iceland, Brazil, Haiti, West Africa, and the United States before reaching the cinematic screen in George Romero's 1968 film, *Night of the Living Dead*. You might think these creatures first launched into the public arena in the 1932 movie, *White Zombie,* starring Béla Lugosi, or the 1936 film, *Revolt of the Zombies.* But in truth, the macabre roots of the zombie legend began long, long ago, in an age when all our stories were told in whispers, when men and women crouched in fear of the capricious gods they worshipped.

Back to the Past

The zombie legend began with legendary beings: the gods of ancient Greece, Egypt, and Sumeria. In the ancient world, it was believed that only a god could travel the distance from death to life. Like forbidden fruit, this was not the stuff of mortals. In Greek legends, love drove Orpheus on his journey to the underworld, where he tried to rescue his dead wife, Eurydice. He almost succeeded in bringing her back but failed by disobeying Hades' orders and glancing back at his wife before she crossed into the upper world. A somewhat similar Egyptian love-story-wrapped-in-myth tells of the god Osiris, murdered by his brother Set, then magically resurrected by his sister and wife, Isis. As time passed and this story was retold, it metamorphosed, first granting immortality to Egyptian kings, and then later, in the New Kingdom era (16th century B.C. to the 11th century B.C.) to all people who knew and performed the proper rituals.

This is the twisted path legends often take, changing slightly with each retelling.

As time passed, stories began to spread throughout the world about others who had returned from the dead. From the Sumerian tales of the god/king Tammuz rescued from the underworld by Inanna to the Hebrew Old Testament stories of Elijah and Elisha raising children from the dead to the Celtic ceremonial slaying of an aging king in the belief that his spirit would then inhabit a younger king, death was now seen as a door that could swing both ways.

Unfortunately, once it began to swing open, what walked through wasn't always friendly.

Common Ancestors

Today, those of us living in the Western world view ghosts as insubstantial and without substance. But this wasn't always the case. This particular viewpoint of spirits didn't become popular until the Victorian era. Before that, the returning dead were believed to be corporeal creatures with the ability to do harm or good—although they seemed to opt for harm more often.

In Romania, these creatures were called *moroi* (benevolent spirits), or *strigoi* (malevolent spirits). When believed to be departed family members, these emissaries of the returning dead were often invited into homes and given a meal. This particular wraith is a common ancestor to both vampires and zombies. In Iceland, the Vikings believed in *draugars,* corpse-white or coal-black creatures who returned from the grave with malicious intent. Many of the *Sagas of Icelanders* from the 9th to the 14th centuries A.D., like the *Laxdoela* and the *Eyrbyggja* and the *Grettis,* include tales of dead men coming back for vengeance or sport. It was believed that the draugar could eat the flesh and drink the blood of their victims.

During the 12th to the 15th century, both England and Germany joined in on the telling of tales, with medieval ghost stories written by monks, courtiers, and churchmen. English writers included William of Newburgh (1136-1198), a Yorkshire canon who wrote that ghosts attacked people and drank their blood, and the 14th-century monk of Byland Abbey who wrote of James Tankerlay, an infamous ghost who returned from the grave to attack his former concubine. Walter Map (1140-1210), courtier of King Henry II of England, wrote some of the earliest vampire stories, while his contemporary, William of Newburgh (1136-1198) wrote of medieval revenants, corpses that returned from the grave.

At this point, the door to the world of the dead no longer swung open on occasion. It had been left ajar. These ghosts and spirits of written folklore had physical bodies—they could eat meals, drink alcohol, and get in fights with humans. Like disobedient children, they refused to stay in the tomb at night, preferring to carouse and stir up trouble. Consequently, their rotting bodies were often exhumed, then burned, staked, or chopped in bits, sometimes replete with a ceremonial beheading, similar to what we associate with vampires today.

Cannot Rest in Peace

By the 1800s, another phenomenon began to stir the imagination and, subsequently, found its way into the pages of literature: Catalepsy, a physical condition that produces muscular rigidity and an appearance similar to death. Today, doctors believe catalepsy is associated with catatonic schizophrenia. Unfortunately, this condition went undiagnosed and untreated in the 19th century and because of it many sufferers went to an early grave—while still alive. Tormented by this fear, Edgar Allan Poe wrote *The Premature Burial* and *The Fall of the House of Usher.* This affliction also found its way into stories by Alexandre Dumas: *The Count of Monte Cristo;* Arthur Conan Doyle: *The Adventure of the Resident Patient;* and George Elliot: *Silas Marner.*

Real tales of catalepsy circulated as well.

In the late 1800s, a woman named Constance Whitney perished, or so it seemed. While still in her coffin, a sexton tried to pry off one of her rings. He accidentally cut her finger with a blade. At this point, she woke up, gave an audible sigh, and then went on to live for several years. A similar tale arises from Northern Ireland, where the body of a wealthy woman was exhumed by thieves. While attempting to steal one of her rings, the "dead" woman revived.

The terms "undead" and "back from the dead" began to take on new meanings. The line between life and death was blurring, setting the stage for the final act in this monster's journey.

Voodoo

In the late 18th century, a Haitian slave uprising and a spirit-based belief system known as voodoo worked together to create an atmosphere of danger and dark magic—the perfect ingredients for the zombie myth to flourish. This belief system traveled from the tribal villages of Africa to the sugarcane plantations of the Caribbean, assimilating many Catholic customs along the way. It took root in Haiti (then known as Saint-Domingue), an island where the slaves soon outnumbered their owners by 10 to 1. Ultimately, voodoo became a political device with "priests"—or *houngan*—urging their followers to war against their owners. For some time, the Caribbean plantation owners worried that their slaves might rebel—a fear that manifested itself in Haiti in 1791. In this uprising, two different island voodoo traditions, Petro and Rada, joined forces, targeting the *petit blancs* and the plantation owners. These uprisings continued until 1804, when Haiti became an independent republic.

Fear played a large part in the 13-year revolution, and as a result, zombie myths began to circulate throughout the Caribbean and France. Outrageous stories were told about how the local Haitian *houngan* employed dark magic to raise the dead, thus creating their own soldiers to war against the militia. Rumors of cannibalism spread as well. Initially, these rumors were created to cause animosity toward the local Creoles and to help quell the rebellion.

Oddly enough, these rumors were the labor pangs that would give birth to the monster that now lumbers across our modern cinema.

The Zombie Slave

Voodoo legends continued into the 19th century, claiming that either a *bokor,* a *houngan,* or a *mambo* could raise the dead and make them do their bidding. Since that time, stories have been told of mindless victims found years after their supposed deaths, stories like the Haitian tale, later proven false, of Felicia Felix-Mentor, allegedly found wandering about in a trance-like state 30 years after her burial. Or the tale of Clairvius Narcisse, who supposedly died in Deschapelles, Haiti, on May 2, 1962, and was later found, alive, in a village in 1980. Narcisse claimed that a bokor had given him a *poudre.* After this, doctors declared him dead, Narcisse was buried, and later "resurrected." Drugs given to him on a regular basis had allegedly numbed his senses and turned him into a zombie, after which he was sold as a slave to work on a sugarcane plantation.

Hoping to discover a new medicine, Dr. Wade Davis spent years investigating the various zombie powders used by bokors, then recorded his findings in *The Serpent and the Rainbow and The Passage of Darkness.* Davis concluded that a drug, or several drugs combined, had caused Narcisse's condition. His theory, based on samples collected while in Haiti, stated that bokors combined tetrodotoxin (from puffer fish), toxins from marine toads, various lizards and spiders, human remains, and sometimes even ground glass to create the powder used in their rituals. Despite Davis' research, the drug used to turn Narcisse into a zombie was never scientifically documented or proven.

Nonetheless, by this time, zombies had already achieved a level of notoriety, becoming the monster muse for both screenwriters and novelists. In 1929, W.B. Seabrook led the pack with *Magic Island,* a steamy voodoo tale set in turn-of-the-century Haiti. A flurry of movies followed that captured the essence of the voodoo zombie slave: *White Zombie* in 1932; *Ouanga* in 1936; *Revolt of the Zombies* in 1936; and *I Walked with a Zombie* in 1943. Then the mood changed in 1968 with the cult classic film, *Night of the Living Dead,* when George Romero introduced new elements: cannibalism, science fiction, and the zombie apocalypse. Heavily influenced by *I Am Legend,* the 1954 vampire novel by Richard Matheson, Romero's tale no longer relied on voodoo or sorcery to raise the dead. Likewise, today, the modern zombie often bears the scars of science gone wrong, with resurrection caused by anything from outer space radiation to toxic gas to an incurable virus to a mysterious cell phone signal. Like the birth of Mary Shelley's masterpiece, you can almost smell the electricity crackle as new ideas emerge. The legend continues to change with each retelling, as new books and movies grant the undead zombie new abilities—now he's agile, now he's intelligent, now he wants equal rights.

At this point, the zombie-returned-from-the-dead can be worked into almost story or portrait. From Jane Austen and Seth Grahame-Smith's *Pride and Prejudice with Zombies* to Max Brook's *World War Z,* the grave is the limit.

It's time to start digging.

Anatomy of a Monster

Classic zombies walk with a shuffling gait, all limbs stiff, movement awkward, laborious and slow. The stumbling corpse out for revenge may have originated in Boris Karloff's interpretation of another monster in the cult-favorite 1932 movie: *The Mummy.*

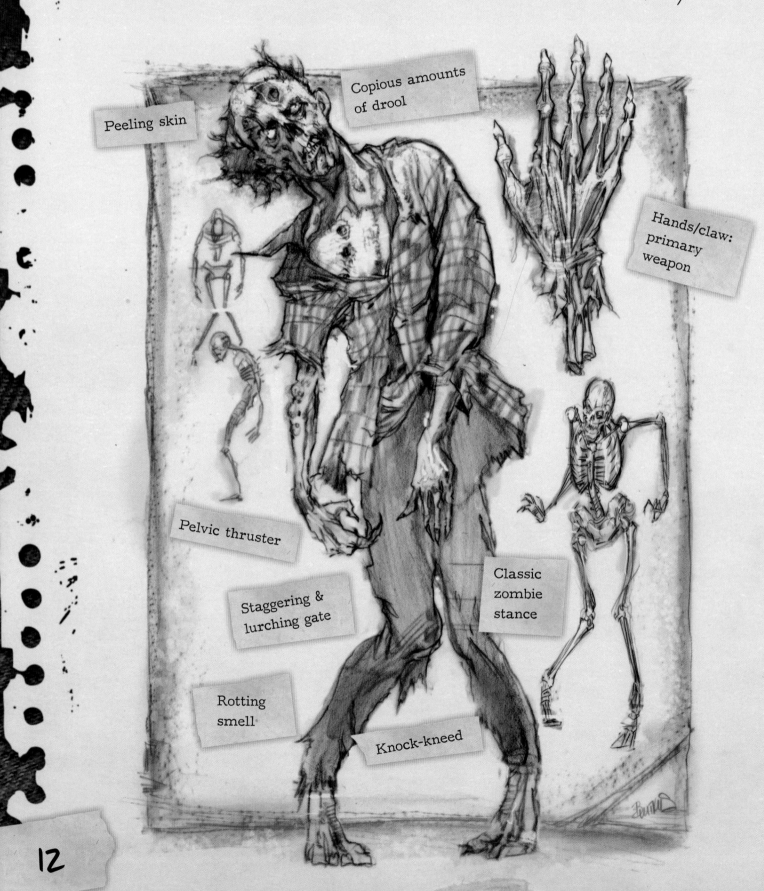

Peeling skin

Copious amounts of drool

Hands/claw: primary weapon

Pelvic thruster

Staggering & lurching gate

Classic zombie stance

Rotting smell

Knock-kneed

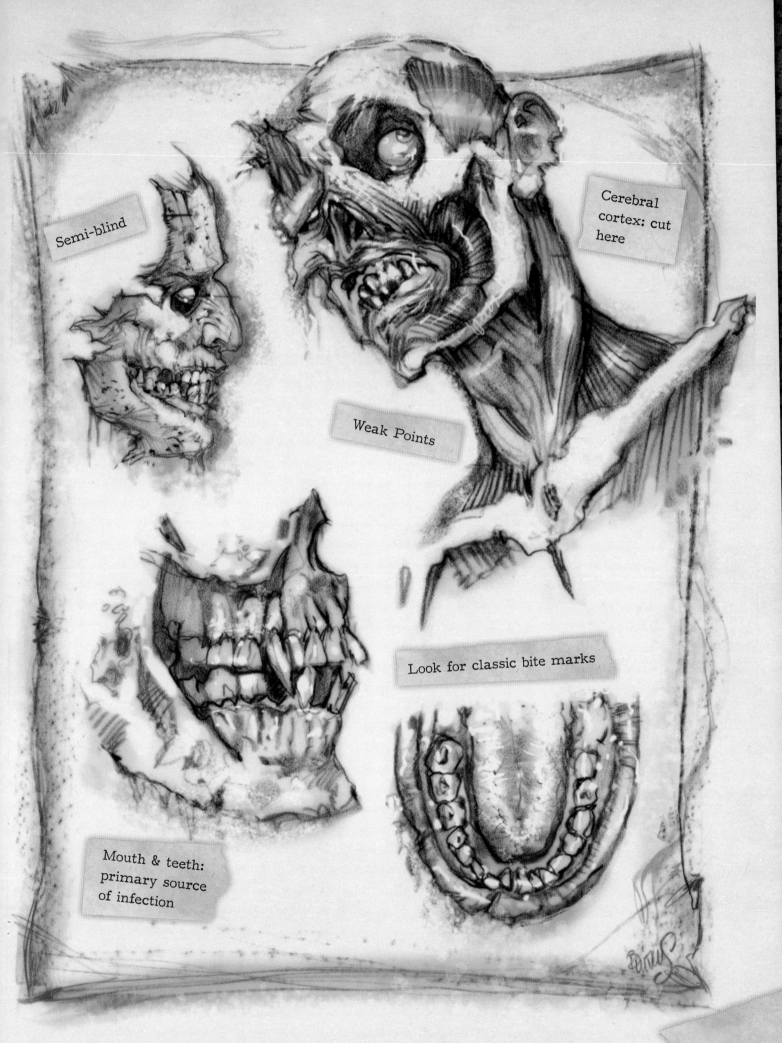

13

Focusing on the Features

Every zombie starts as a normal human, then swiftly transforms from gorgeous to gruesome. To create your own undead monster, remember to pay close attention to the bone structure of your character. As the skin decays, all sorts of skeletal anatomy, sagging flesh, and broken bones will be exposed.

Eyes

Eyes say a lot about a person, or creature, so use this as an opportunity to express the true nature of your character. Begin by drawing a ball—this will remind you to "wrap" your lines and values around a 3-dimensional form. For an attractive human eye, the iris will remain centered in the white when it looks at you, leaving just a bit of space between it and the bottom lid. For the zombie eye, move the iris so far up that only the bottom half shows. Then, draw in extra creases and wrinkles on the top and bottom lids, showing that the zombie has been missing his beauty sleep. Also, for a gruesome touch, you can add additional fluid and goo leaking from the inside of the eye. For a more wicked zombie, simply pull down the top lid, narrowing the inner canthus into a skinny slit.

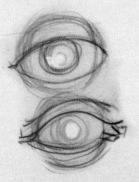

Hands

As the flesh of the hand begins to disintegrate, you'll find that the ligaments and bones create a network of long, thin lines. Keep the fingers curled and the tips pointed for good measure.

Nose

When drawing the zombie facial features, start with a generic drawing of a human face. For example, a normal nose has a bottom that typically runs parallel to the floor. In contrast, when drawing a zombie, give it a severe pug nose by pulling the nostrils up high and flattening the apex. For the zombie's mouth, pull the lips back to reveal crooked and deformed teeth.

Zombie Evolution

The classic zombie no longer dominates the landscape in monster lore. Today new variations continually spring up, like corroded links in an evolutionary chain gone awry. Tattered skin and exposed bone may always be in vogue, but the rest of the zombie package is open for interpretation.

Walking upright is still an effort

Hunting for food

Back from the grave

Primal thoughts

Perfecting the shuffle

Pack mentality

Catching the waves between bites

Technology to the rescue

Survival of the fittest and meanest

17

Survival Tactics

In every good zombie story, there comes a point where running away from the monster just isn't enough. The bad guy needs to be destroyed. Unless you set him on fire, this undead creature will only return to the crypt if his head is blown off, cut off, or crushed. That means your protagonist will need an arsenal of guns, knives, or hatchets if he hopes to live.

Here we see some of the more effective weapons that have been used to dispatch the local zombie over the years. As with any drawing, start off with the simplest of shapes that represent the subject, for example, circles, cylinders, and rectangles. Keep the following three things in mind when creating believable weapons or gadgets:

- Number one: Keep the lines crisp and clean.
- Number two: Always imagine the forms are solid masses so that you can shade and add value accordingly.
- Number three: The perspective must be accurate. As long as the perspective is correct, you can exaggerate the foreshortening, making the drawing more dynamic.

Setting the Stage

Background elements play a major role in making your zombie illustration look real. Spooky details, like a menacing tree or a creepy spider, help to make your imaginary world more real. Tombstones and crypts, the resting places that all zombies have forsaken, provide visual reminders that these creatures have supernaturally risen from the grave.

Tree

Next, we're going to create a tree that would look perfect on a zombie's front yard. Begin with some simple linear shapes for the trunk. We're going to draw a very human-like form, reminiscent of the trees from your childhood nightmares. Once you're satisfied with the line drawing, add some organic curves and folds to the tree, similar to what you would find on a long robe. Leave the branches bare and keep the ends sharp, like claws. We want this tree to have a form similar to that of a headless zombie.

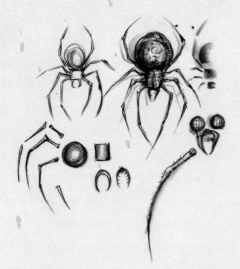

Spider

Incredibly easy to draw, spiders add a whimsical, yet eerie, touch to an illustration. Begin with basic shapes to put together a recognizable form of a spider. Keep the tips of their legs razor-sharp to give them a dangerous edge. Finally, add some extra hair to the legs and abdomen of these terrifying critters and you're done.

Tombstones and Graves

Now we'll focus on the birthplace of the zombie—the gravesite. Start off with basic block shapes. If desired, you can do a little research on old tombstones first. When drawing, make sure your lines are clean and the perspective is accurate. Add some different textures like cracks and smudges to create a grittier, dirtier feel. You can also put sandpaper beneath the drawing when you do the shading to add to the texture.

Drawing Materials

Drawing zombies is a bit simpler than painting or rendering them on the computer, so let's start here. Basically, drawing consists of indicating shapes and defining values (the lightness or darkness of a color or of black). Because one relies so heavily on value to represent the subject, it's important to include a range of values for variety and contrast. Keep this in mind throughout your drawing process—from the beginning stages to the final details.

Drawing pencil

Colored pencils

Charcoal Pencil

Indelible Marker

Paintbrushes

Acrylic Paints

Materials Checklist

To complete all the drawing projects in this book, you'll need to purchase the materials below. Note that the exact materials needed for each project are listed at the start of each project:

- Multimedia vellum paper (9" x 12")
- Gessoed two-ply white illustration board (8.5" x 11")
- Tracing paper (15" x 20")
- Raw white illustration board (8.5" x 11")
- #2 (HB) pencil
- Kneaded eraser
- Pencil sharpener
- 600-grit sandpaper
- Colored pencils: black, white, 30% gray, 30% cool gray
- Black charcoal pencil
- Black indelible felt pen
- Gouache paints: lamp black and permanent white
- Acrylic paints: Payne's gray and Mars black
- #5 paintbrush (medium)
- #00 paintbrush (very small)
- Old toothbrush
- Workable spray fixative
- Airbrush (optional)
- Computer system, digital pen/graphic tablet, and Photoshop® (all optional; see page 101)

Light Table

The projects in this book will be easiest if you have access to a light table, such as the one shown on the right. This illuminated surface makes it possible to create a clean outline from a sketch, simply by placing a sheet of paper over your sketch and tracing. If you don't have a light table, you'll want to keep your initial sketch lines very light so they can be erased at a later stage.

Pencils

Graphite drawing pencils are generally graphite "leads" encased in wood. The lead comes in grades and is usually accompanied by a letter ("H" for "hard," or "B" for "soft") and a number (ranging from 2 to 9). The higher the number accompanying the letter, the harder or softer the graphite. (For example, a 9B pencil is extremely soft.) Hard pencils produce a light value and can score the surface of the paper, whereas softer pencils produce darker values and smudge easily. For this reason, stick to an HB (aka #2) pencil, which is right in between hard and soft pencils.

In addition to graphite pencils, you will also use a charcoal and a few colored pencils. Charcoal, (made up of burnt wood), is a dark, rich medium that can give a drawing dramatic contrast. Be careful—it smears easily! Colored pencils are less likely to smear and come in a wide range of colors. (See also "Colored Pencils" on page 65.)

Kneaded Eraser

A kneaded eraser is a helpful tool that can serve as both an eraser and a drawing tool. It can be molded into any shape, making it easy to remove graphite from your drawing surface. To erase, simply press the kneaded eraser onto your paper and lift. Unlike kneaded erasers, rubber or vinyl erasers can damage delicate drawing surfaces, and it's not as easy to be precise.

Paints

The project in this chapter involve mostly drawing, but they do suggest paint to accent areas here and there. The gouache (an opaque type of watercolor) and acrylic paints listed are all water-soluble, so you'll need a jar of water and some paper towels when using them. You can use either natural or synthetic hair bristles with gouache paint, but you'll want to stick with synthetic bristles when using acrylic.

Workable Spray Fixative

Coating your drawings with a layer of spray fixative can help prevent smudging as you develop your drawings. It's easy—especially while using charcoal—to accidentally smear your strokes. Workable spray fixative allows you to spray occasionally throughout your drawing process, so you can prevent accidents along the way.

Drawing Surfaces

Traditional drawing paper comes in three types: hot-press (smooth), cold-press (textured), and rough. Choose your texture according to your desired look. In general, rough paper produces broken strokes; it's not conducive to creating detail, but it's ideal for a sketchy style. Smooth paper allows for smooth, controlled strokes. In this chapter, the projects call for vellum paper and illustration board, which offer suitable surfaces for a multimedia drawing approach.

Zombie Beauty Queen

For the average glamour girl, beauty is only skin deep. Not so for the zombie— for her it goes all the way to the bone. In a zombie beauty contest, gore, sinew, and rotting flesh are all part of the pageant, so this project focuses on the contrast between earthly beauty and disgusting decomposition.

Materials
- Multimedia vellum paper (9" x 12")
- Kneaded eraser
- #2 pencil
- Black colored pencil
- 30% cool gray colored pencil
- 600-grit sandpaper
- Photoshop® (optional)

▲ **Step One** Plan your portrait with a rough sketch, working out the pose and the general value distribution.

Step Two Once you're satisfied with the concept of your thumbnail, begin a linear drawing on vellum paper. At this early stage, make sure that the features are positioned properly. (You can transfer this sketch; see "Transferring a Drawing" on page 25.)

Step Three After the drawing is complete and you're happy with the proportions, immediately start on the distorted zombie features. Use the black colored pencil at this point.

TRANSFERRING A DRAWING

To begin the projects in this book, you might find it helpful to trace a basic outline of the final piece of art (or one of the early steps). Transferring the outlines of an image to your drawing or painting surface is easier than you may think. The easiest method for this involves transfer paper, which you can buy at your local arts and crafts store. Transfer paper is a thin sheet of paper that is coated on one side with graphite. (You can also create your own version of transfer paper by covering one side of a piece of paper with graphite from a pencil.) Simply follow the steps below.

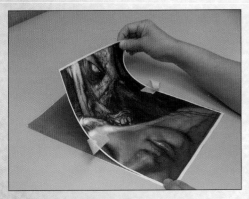

Step 1 Make a photocopy of the image you would like to transfer and enlarge it to the size of your drawing paper or canvas. Place the transfer paper graphite-side-down over your paper or canvas. Then place your photocopy over the transfer paper and secure them in place.

Step 2 Lightly trace the lines that you would like to transfer onto your drawing or painting surface. When transferring a guide for a drawing project, keep the lines minimal and just indicate the position of each element; you don't want to have to erase too much once you remove the transfer paper.

Step 3 While tracing, occasionally lift the corner of the photocopy to make sure the lines are transferring properly. Continue tracing over the photocopy until all of your lines have been transferred.

▶ **Step Four** It's extremely important to keep your pencils sharp, especially when drawing at this size and when using vellum paper. It's best to use an electric sharpener that produces very sharp tips (preferably to a 16-degree point). Next, use 600-grit sandpaper to further sharpen the pencil. This also creates a chiseled edge which makes it easier to vary the width of your line as you draw.

◀ **Step Five** Next, start adding tone and detail to the structure on the zombie side of the vixen's face, making sure that it looks believable.

25

Step Six At this point, you want to set up the values for the next stage of the drawing. It's incredibly important to be aware of your line quality and design of shape as you move into each step of your illustration.

Step Seven Once some of the twisted facial features of the zombie have been laid in, move on to the human features. Slowly build up the values on the skin tone, using a 30% cool gray colored pencil. Again, remember to keep it very sharp. Use a rubber pencil eraser to pick out highlights that will accent the facial structure.

Step Eight After finishing the softer features of your sexy zombie vixen, focus on creating a sense of depth by showing different textures of human anatomy such as bones, flesh, and brain matter. Then, start the process of integrating these textures into wonderfully horrific, yet well-designed shapes.

GREAT ZOMBIE READS

You don't want to feel left out the next time your friends are discussing zombies. The below list can help you brush up on zombie lore, and teach you how to survive if the great zombie apocalypse unfolds sooner than expected.

Books:
Magic Island: 1929 by W.B. Seabrook
The Rising; City of the Dead: both by Brian Keene
Cell: 2006 by Stephen King
World War Z: 2007 by Max Brooks
The Zombie Survival Guide: 2003 by Max Brooks
Zombie Haiku: 2008 by Ryan Mecum
Pride and Prejudice and Zombies: 2009 by Jane Austen and Seth Grahame-Smith
Monster Island; Monster Nation; Monster Planet: all by David Wellington
The Restless Dead: 2003 by Hugh B. Cave

Comics/Graphic Novels:
Dark Horse Comics ZombieWorld: Champion of the Worms by Mike Mignola and Pat McEown
Dawn of the Dead adaptation by Steve Niles and Chee
Marvel Comics miniseries: Marvel Zombies
Arrow Comics: Deadworld
Image Comics: The Walking Dead

Step Nine At this point, we have completed the drawing. However, you may want to follow the next four steps to give your work a little digital enhancement. Begin this stage by scanning the drawing and bringing it into image-editing software, such as Photoshop®.

28

Step Ten This is my studio setup. On the left, I have both my reference material and the beginning stages of the drawing. I work off the middle screen, and refer to the original as I work.

▼ **Step Eleven** Next, using the levels tool (page 101), darken the whole illustration by about 20%. This immediately gives the mid value we need without spending a lot of time darkening the actual drawing. Then use the eraser tool with a soft edge (page 101) to bring out the highlights.

Note: I have added spots of rotting flesh over the shoulder and chest. The great part about adding details digitally is that you can be experimental; your changes are not permanent, so long as you don't save over the original scan!

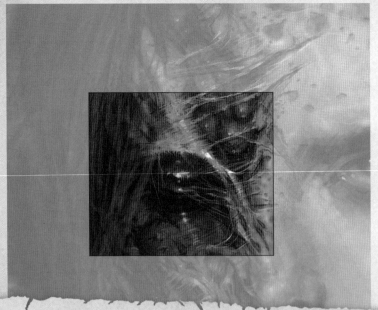

Step Twelve
Use the eraser tool to pull out strings of flesh on the zombie side of the face. You can also use the eraser tool to create some energy and texture in the hair and skin, thus giving a frenzied look to our zombie beauty.

Step Thirteen Next, use the dodge tool (page 101). Select the highlight as the range and bring out the highlights of the eyes, the flesh, and the lips to make them appear wet. Adjust the diameter and exposure of your tool as necessary.

▶ **Step Fourteen** Again using the dodge tool, blow out the background — only use a much bigger diameter this time. This will bring the zombie forward and provide a more exciting contrast. Once all this is done, use the blur tool to soften the edges and create an almost photographic quality. In this illustration, 90% of the drawing was done traditionally, while only the last ten minutes were spent on the computer.

ZOMBIE LAW

Whether part of the on-going legend or actual historic fact, the possibility of a Haitian law against creating zombies certainly adds fuel to the folklore fire. Supposedly put into effect in 1835, the Haitian Penal Code, Article 249, made its way into the book, White Zombie: Anatomy of a Horror Film by Gary Don Rhodes. Below is a quote:

"Haitian Penal Code: Article 249. It shall also be qualified as attempted murder the employment which may be made against any person of substances which, without causing actual death, produce a lethargic coma more or less prolonged. If, after the person had been buried, the act shall be considered murder no matter what result follows."

31

Grave Zombie

You can accomplish a lot with a little help from your friends. Here we see a zombie escaping from the grave, watched over by a crowd of his undead pals. This black and white illustration will focus on how to create a dynamic composition.

Materials
- Gessoed two-ply white illustration board (8.5" x 11")
- Black indelible felt pen
- Lamp black gouache
- Permanent white gouache
- Colored pencils: black, white, & 30% gray
- #5 brush
- #00 brush
- #2 pencil
- Old toothbrush

Step One This is the thumbnail for our next illustration in which we will be focusing on dynamic composition.

Step Two This project involves a fun and quick technique. On a gessoed board, start the drawing with a #2 pencil, basing it on the composition of the thumbnail. (You can transfer this sketch; see "Transferring a Drawing" on page 25.)

Step Three With your line drawing in place, use the black felt pen to go over the drawing, making sure your lines and shapes are exciting and full of energy.

▲ Step Four Diluting your lamp black gouache with a good amount of water, quickly brush in a dark value around the grave and zombies.

▶ Step Five When you've finished with the gouache, take your illustration outside and lightly spray it with workable fixative. Once dry (about 10 minutes), dip an old toothbrush in the black gouache and splatter the paint all over the drawing, immediately creating new textures. Then hit it once more with a little workable fixative.

▲ **Step Six** Using my 30% gray pencil, start bringing out the teeth, face, and strands of hair. Be sure to emphasize the stretching and pulling of the taut dead flesh by using thinner lines over the dark shapes. Also start working on the sky by mixing some white gouache with water and painting around the silhouettes of the distant zombies.

▶ **Step Seven** With the #5 brush, dip it lightly in the white mixture and paint in some soft, fuzzy shapes for the hair, emphasizing the dry, frizzy texture.

Step Eight Switching over to the very small detailing brush (size #00), start adding highlights along the left side of the face. Then paint in a rim light along the edge of his hair and shoulders to suggest the light source from the sky and to separate the main character from the background.

Step Nine Now it's time to work on the zombie onlookers. Still using the fine brush, quickly block in the big shapes of the skeletal faces and indicate the light source by painting a rim light around the body of the standing zombie.

Note: You'll see that the project strayed from the thumbnail; the outside zombies have changed. I constantly play and experiment with my characters and composition throughout the process. Remember, this is from your imagination. Don't be afraid to explore for a more successful composition.

Teenage Zombie Killer

Buffy the Vampire Slayer has nothing on this teenage high school student, ready to single-handedly take on a zombie horde. This is a heroine worthy of her own graphic novel, and her innocence makes a nice contrast with the monsters she battles.

Materials
- Black colored pencil
- 30% cool gray pencil
- Multimedia vellum paper (9" x 12")
- Tracing paper (15" x 20")

▲ **Step One** We begin the project by working out the sketch on tracing paper.

▶ **Step Two** Once you're happy with your concept, transfer the image onto vellum paper. (See "Transferring a Drawing" on page 25.) Then, create a linear sketch using a black colored pencil. Once complete, block in the dark values on the zombie heads in the locker, using smooth and consistent strokes. To add more depth to these shadowy areas, start putting in some darker accents. For example, focus on the eye sockets, the insides of the mouths and corners of the eyes. Note: Always keep your pencil sharp when drawing on vellum. You can keep another 20 or so sheets of vellum under your illustration to give your pencil a slight bounce and the drawing a "creamy" texture.

Step Three Once the three main values have been established, begin to work on the teenage zombie killer. Draw a holding line around her to give this illustration a comic book feel. Since she is supposed to be young and pretty, the less you do, the better she will look. Concentrate on designing attractive lines and shapes. Keep the values light with the exception of some accents in the eyes and the corners of the mouth.

Step Four For this step, continue the holding line down the rest of her body, varying the quality of the line from thick to thin to suggest form. The line is just as important as value and shape in sustaining the energy of any drawing.

HOW TO TELL IF YOUR BEST FRIEND IS A ZOMBIE

1. She walks with a shuffle.
2. She doesn't cry when her boyfriend breaks up with her.
3. His hair starts to fall out in clumps and his breath smells worse than ever.
4. He's hungry all the time, but never wants to go out for pizza. Even if you're buying.
5. She offers to bury your dead cat. But your cat isn't dead.
6. She starts to say things like, "Aaaaarrrrrrrrggggg" and "Uuummmmppppphh."
7. He can't remember the answers in Algebra. Doesn't even remember what Algebra is.
8. One of his fingers falls off while he's writing notes.
9. She starts to hang out with a different crowd. They all stare at you and drool when you walk past.
10. She breaks into your house at midnight and tries to eat your little brother.

Step Five Now it's time to start adding the lines and shapes that create the folds of her clothes and her textbook. Once she is complete, switch to your gray pencil and put in a very light value for her skin. To add some gore to the environment, use a black pencil to indicate blood dripping down the locker doors, making sure you follow what would be the curvature of the metal. Note: Even though this is a gory scene, don't let it become sloppy. Try to keep your shading clean and consistent.

Step Six In this last stage, look over your drawing and fine-tune any detail you may have overlooked. If you study it closely, you'll note that this illustration is mostly linear and has very few values. Because of this, the placement of the dark accents and the holding line are very important — otherwise, the drawing may appear unfinished.

Snowboarding Zombie

Every teenager loves extreme sports, and the zombie teen is no exception. This illustration focuses on how to convey energy, body language, and dynamic composition.

Materials
- Black colored pencil
- Kneaded eraser
- #2 pencil
- Multimedia vellum paper
- Computer system and Photoshop® (optional)

▶ **Step One** We begin this project with a rough line drawing of a zombie snowboarder.

Step Two With a sharp #2 pencil, create the sketch for the final drawing on vellum paper. Note that the original sketch has been changed; now the skull is staring off into the distance, instead of facing the viewer like the zombie. (You can transfer this sketch; see "Transferring a Drawing" on page 25.)

▶ **Step Three** Begin working on the skull. Shade in all the shadow areas and make sure the shapes are clear and well-designed. Exaggerating the size and the shapes on the skull will emphasize its wicked expression. Also, add some quick little nicks and scratches to show that it's been through some tough times. Then, make the hair look almost like wisps of smoke to convey a sense of movement. Next, start putting the darks on the face of the killer airborne zombie. Then, begin to shade all the big shapes of the clothes. Although this is a fast process, make sure your strokes are smooth, consistent, and clean. You don't want this area to distract the viewer. Once you have established the middle value, start laying in the darks of the folds and creases. Notice that the shapes are strong and stylized. You can look through fashion magazines or photograph a model to make sure the folds of the fabric look realistic.

Step Four This is the stage where the drawing really starts to get exciting. At this point, the personality emerges, almost as if the character is jumping out at you. The fact that the image breaks the frames gives the drawing a dynamic energy. Remember, you don't have to confine yourself to four corners; instead, use them to your advantage. Add some tattoo art on the zombie's arm to show what his personal style was before he became one of the undead. Also, emphasize the zombie's crouching position by pushing his body back into a darker value. Now, move on to the intricate designs of the snowboard. Just because the snowboard designs look intricate doesn't mean they will take a long time. As long as you keep your line quality clean and varied, and the shapes strong and attractive, it will appear that you spent more time than you actually did.

Step Five Here you can see an example of breaking frame, as discussed in Step Four. Add external elements like flying snow and make sure they bleed off the edges. Having the snow weave in and out of the composition helps to create a sense of action.

Step Six Continue building values throughout the drawing and adding a few sprays of snow here and there. With the drawing complete, the next several steps are optional and involve working on a computer. For this part of the process, we first scan it into Photoshop®, then put in a few highlights, and do a little clean up. This process should take only about 10 minutes.

46

Step Seven Enlarge the drawing to find any areas that need attention.

Step Eight I have a Wacom Cintiq—a screen that you can actually draw on. Once my drawing is on the Cintiq, I use the stylus pen and select the airbrush tool from Photoshop®'s tool bar. From the palette, select a medium-light gray, and then start to soften edges and intensify some of the darks. (See page 101.)

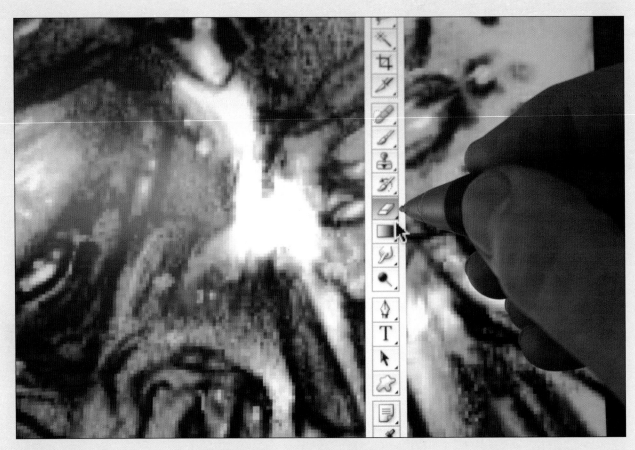

Step Nine The eraser tool is extremely useful for brightening highlights, softening edges, and removing any extraneous lines. You can adjust the width, opacity, and softness of the eraser.

Step Ten In this step, you can see how much detail can be added to a relatively small drawing (6" x 10") in a short period of time by using Photoshop®.

49

Misty Grave Zombie

You just can't keep a good man down—especially when he's a zombie. Here we see the decomposing monster returning from the grave. Special effects, created with an airbrush and Photoshop®, add just the right touch of supernatural light and fog.

Materials
- Acrylic paint: Titanium white, Payne's gray, Mars black
- Small acrylic paintbrush
- Raw white illustration board (8.5" x 11")
- Black colored pencil
- White colored pencil
- Black charcoal pencil
- Kneaded eraser
- Workable spray fixative
- Airbrush (optional)
- Computer system and Photoshop® (optional)

▲ **Step One** Begin with a sketch that engages the viewer. Make it look as though the zombie is climbing out of the grave and off the picture toward the viewer.

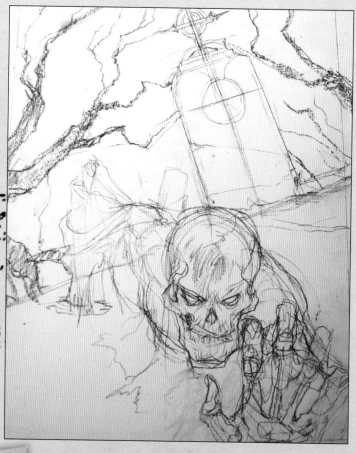

Step Two On a raw white illustration board, begin a fresh drawing with a black charcoal pencil. (You can transfer this sketch; see "Transferring a Drawing" on page 25.)

Step Three To achieve the effect of a creepy, foggy grave site, smudge the charcoal with your fingers, still keeping a light value of the drawing intact.

▲ **Step Four** After smudging the background, begin to pick out the highlights with the kneaded eraser.

◀ **Step Five** Next, take the drawing outside and spray a light layer of workable spray fixative to seal it. Once it is completely dry, begin drawing back into the illustration using a black colored pencil. This process will enhance the line quality.

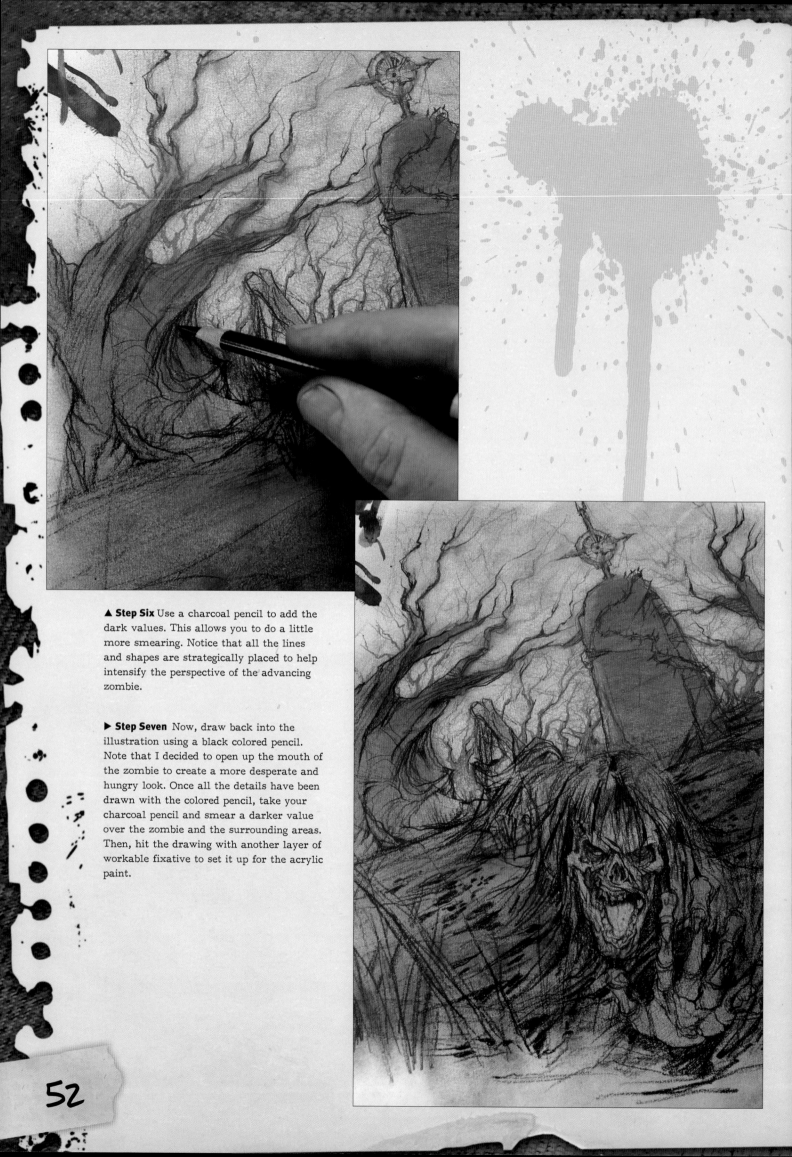

▲ Step Six Use a charcoal pencil to add the dark values. This allows you to do a little more smearing. Notice that all the lines and shapes are strategically placed to help intensify the perspective of the advancing zombie.

▶ Step Seven Now, draw back into the illustration using a black colored pencil. Note that I decided to open up the mouth of the zombie to create a more desperate and hungry look. Once all the details have been drawn with the colored pencil, take your charcoal pencil and smear a darker value over the zombie and the surrounding areas. Then, hit the drawing with another layer of workable fixative to set it up for the acrylic paint.

52

Step Eight Using just a white colored pencil, brighten up the horizon and give the zombie a rim light to separate him from the background.

◄ **Step Nine** To create the mist, get out your airbrush and fill it with a little titanium white acrylic paint mixed with water. With the exception of the zombie's face, give the whole illustration a light spray. Then, with a small brush, use some Payne's gray and a little titanium white for the transitional values between the mist and the zombie. Note: An airbrush is the best tool for creating a misty effect. However, you can use very thin washes of white paint, blending away any hard edges with water.

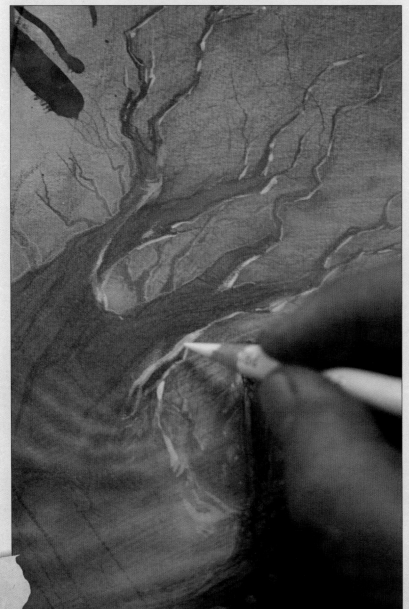

◄ **Step Ten** After you're finished with the airbrush, take a white colored pencil and redefine both the rim lighting and highlights.

▶ **Step Eleven** To make the crawling zombie pop out of the environment a bit more, mix a little bit of Mars black and a lot of water, and then lightly paint him with a thin layer of the wash. Then scan the illustration into Photoshop®. Using the dodge tool (see page 101), quickly intensify the highlights and adjust the levels to create a bit more contrast.

55

A.T.M. Zombie

This project features a black-and-white illustration that could fit into multiple genres: cartoon, comic book, graphic novel, or editorial commentary. Out for an afternoon shopping spree, this suburban zombie couple is shown attempting to withdraw some cash from the local A.T.M. machine.

Materials
- Tracing paper
- Vellum paper
- Kneaded eraser
- Black colored pencil

▲ **Step One** The process begins with a thumbnail sketch. Note that the design often changes from one step to the next. This is all part of the natural evolution of an illustration.

Step Two Block in your drawing using a black colored pencil on tracing paper. You can be as sketchy as you'd like at this point; this project focuses on the process of refining a sketch and stylizing your strokes.

Step Three Here we see part of the design evolution in progress. There needed to be a greater size difference between the male character and his lady friend. The male character was erased with a kneaded eraser and then transformed into a "muscle-head boyfriend" for the female zombie. He now hulks outside the frame to emphasize his mass. This is one guy you wouldn't want to rob from at the A.T.M.—assuming he could figure out how to withdraw money in the first place.

Step Four Once you're happy with your sketch, take a sheet of vellum paper and lay it over the block-in for the finished illustration. Using black colored pencil on vellum gives a clean, creamy finish, perfect for the look we want on this drawing. The key here is to keep your pencil extremely sharp.

Step Five Concentrate on the zombie boyfriend first. Emphasize his masculinity by keeping his features angular and by adding facial hair. Also, exaggerate his grimace and frown lines to show that this zombie probably never knew how to operate an A.T.M., dead or alive.

ZOMBIE IN TRAINING

Another infamous tale of catalepsy involved a young lad who lived in Victorian era London. Ernest Wicks first perished in 1895, when he was about 2 years old. During examination at the mortuary, a faint movement was noted in the child's chest. Vigorous rubbing of the boy's arms brought him back to consciousness. By the time Ernest was 13, he had died several more times, and he ended up with at least three death certificates by 1902.

Step Six It's a good idea to compare the sketch with your final drawing from time to time. Do this to see how close your final illustration is to the original lay-in, and to decide whether you want to make any changes. This process will give you a fresh eye.

Step Seven Next, work on the rest of the male zombie's form. Most of his body will in be shadow so we'll be able to see the silhouette of his zombie girlfriend clearly. Add detail to his tattered shirt and some spiky tattoos to his ape-like arm for interest.

◄ **Step Eight** Now, move on to the zombie valley girl. In contrast to her ultra masculine boyfriend, give curves to her skeletal body and add feminine touches like a big bow to her hair and some floral designs to her dress. Vary your line quality from straight to curvy and thick to thin. There won't be a lot of value work to her, so pay special attention to designing her shapes. The contrast between shape, line quality, and value are the keys to making an exciting and successful black-and-white drawing.

▶ **Step Nine** Keep the drawing simple on the A.T.M. machine—you only need to indicate all the buttons and blinking lights. The ATM machine becomes believable if you remember to keep the lines straight and crisp and the perspective accurate. Then, add some more goo and gore to the illustration. Even though this couple's on a shopping spree instead of a killing spree, they're still zombies!

Step Ten For the last step, add some final dark accents to our zombie couple. Notice how this illustration breaks the compositional frame with fun shapes and line texture. Remember, you don't have to think inside the box.

61

Chapter 7:
Painting
Zombies

Painting Materials

Painting is generally more difficult than drawing because, in addition to strokes and values, you must also consider color and its many aspects—saturation, hue, paint mixing, color schemes, etc. By following the projects in this chapter step by step, hopefully you will get ideas for how to approach color and develop your paintings. The focus of this chapter will be on the painting aspect; however, as in Chapter 2, you will have the option of finishing the paintings with a few digital tweaks.

Toothbrush

Acrylic Paints

Drawing pencil

Paint Palette

Materials Checklist

To complete all the painting projects in this book, you'll need to purchase the materials below. Note that the exact materials needed for each project are listed at the start of each project.

- Acrylic paints: Mars black, Payne's Gray, viridian hue permanent, turquoise deep, cerulean blue hue, cadmium red light, cadmium red deep hue, iridescent antique brown, unbleached titanium, phthalocyanine (aka phthalo) blue, Turner's yellow, light portrait pink, naphthol red light, cobalt blue, Hooker's green, burnt umber, acra violet, Prussian blue, cadmium yellow medium, lamp black, portrait pink, titanium white, and cadmium yellow
- Multimedia vellum paper
- White two-ply cold pressed illustration board (15" x 20"; 7" x 15")
- Masonite board (9" x 12")
- #2 (HB) pencil
- 64 or 120 assorted box of colored pencils
- Electric pencil sharpener
- Palette for mixing acrylic paints
- A variety of synthetic brushes ranging from #00 to #6 (very small to medium)
- White and clear gesso
- Matte medium
- Workable spray fixative
- House painting brush
- Old toothbrush
- Window cleaner
- Blowdryer
- Sandpaper (any fine grain will do)
- Airbrush (optional)
- Projector (optional)
- Computer system, digital pen/graphic tablet, and Photoshop® (all optional; see page 101)

64

Acrylic Paint

Acrylic paint is fast-drying paint containing pigment suspended in an acrylic polymer emulsion. Acrylic paints can be diluted with water, but become water-resistant when dry. Depending on how much the paint is diluted (with water) or modified with acrylic gels, media, or pastes, the finished acrylic painting can resemble a watercolor or an oil painting, or have its own unique characteristics not attainable with other media. You can apply acrylic in thin, diluted layers, or apply it in thick, impasto strokes.

Paintbrushes

When using acrylics, we recommend synthetic hair paintbrushes. For the projects in this book, you'll want a variety of sizes, from size 00 (very small) to size 6 (medium). Also consider gathering a variety of bristle shapes. Round brushes have bristles that taper to a point, allowing for a range of stroke sizes. Flat brushes have bristles that are pinched into a squared tip. The flat edge produces thick, uniform lines. In addition to these acrylic brushes, you'll also want a house painting brush—a large paintbrush with coarse bristles. These brushes are perfect for quickly covering the canvas with large washes of color. If you own an airbrush, use this when recommended in the projects, as it produces incredibly soft, realistic gradations that are more difficult to achieve with paintbrushes.

Finding Inspiration

While learning how to draw and paint zombies, it's a good idea to surround yourself with plenty of visual stimulation. An entire corner of my studio is devoted to reference books and props.

Paintbrushes

Colored Pencils

Painting Surfaces

You can use acrylic paint on practically any surface, as long as it's not greasy or waxy. As a result, you have a lot of flexibility with your painting surfaces. However, it's best to paint on either canvas or illustration board coated with a white gesso (a coating used to create an ideal painting surface). Remember that the brighter (or whiter) your painting surface, the more luminous your colors will turn out!

Colored Pencils

Colored pencils aren't just for drawing; they are great tools for adding details to a painting. Working directly over acrylic paint, you can add highlights, intensify shadows, create strands of hair, and more. It's important to purchase the best colored pencils you can afford; higher quality pencils are softer and have more pigment, giving you smoother, easier coverage.

65

Wicked Zombie Portrait

Typically you'd want to put on your best face for a portrait. Not so for the zombie; instead, a portrait provides the perfect opportunity to show off just how terrifying (and disgusting) he can be. With this project, you'll discover that the power of gore lies in the details—from veins and cysts to splatters of blood.

Materials

- Acrylic paints: Naphthol red light, cobalt blue, Hooker's green, burnt umber, acra violet, Prussian blue, cadmium yellow medium, Mars black, lamp black, and light portrait pink (your own preference of warm and cool colors would be fine)
- Vellum paper
- White two-ply cold-pressed illustration board (15" x 20")
- White gesso
- Workable spray fixative
- Window cleaner
- Inexpensive house painting brush
- Palette for acrylic paints
- A variety of acrylic brushes ranging from size #00 to #6
- Electric pencil sharpener
- Cheap toothbrush
- Blowdryer
- Airbrush (optional)
- Projector (optional)
- An assortment of colored pencils
- 600-grit sandpaper (any fine grain will do)

▲ **Step One** Begin by brainstorming possible zombie head poses and angles. For this painting, I want to juxtapose a traditional portrait stance with over-the-top gore, so I choose the brooding, three-quarter view (far left).

▲ **Step Two** To make this zombie to look incredibly wicked, concentrate on the texture. Using the thumbnail as reference, begin the drawing with a black colored pencil on vellum paper. For this project, we'll use a projector to transfer the image to a gessoed illustration board. I recommend that you xerox two copies of your drawing. Place one copy beside your drawing board, and place the other copy above your projection from time to time, making sure that the projected drawing is accurate and not distorted. (You can transfer this sketch; see "Transferring a Drawing" on page 25.)

◄ **Step Three** Begin the painting by placing the following colors on your palette: burnt umber, acra violet, naphthol red light, Hooker's green, Prussian blue, Mars black, lamp black, and cadmium yellow medium. Mix a combination of burnt umber, cadmium yellow medium, and naphthol red light, and then dilute it with plenty of water. Using a big, inexpensive house painting brush, quickly coat the surface, leaving the broad strokes and mottling to dry. For a rapid dry, use a blowdryer. After this, add a thin layer of workable fixative. Now the painting is ready for the next layer of cool transparent color.

► **Step Four** Next, create a mixture of Hooker's green, Prussian blue, and a little lamp black, again diluting it with plenty of water. Using the big brush (rinsed clean), roughly stroke in the cool color around the zombie. The coolness of the background will help the warm head and body of the zombie advance toward the viewer.

◄ **Step Five** Then load your airbrush with a little Mars black and start adding the shadow areas under the nose, the eyes, and the jaw. Shade within the ear and across the scalp. These soft gradations of shadow give the zombie form; you can almost see him start to pop off the page. If you don't have an airbrush, add shadows by building up thin washes of paint, softening the edges by blending in water.

67

▶ **Step Six** Then take a 50/50 mixture of white gesso and water and use it to paint over the background several times, setting it up for the next layer of texture mottling. To get ready for the cool tones of the zombie, clean out your palette and fill it with Hooker's green, Prussian blue, Mars black, cobalt blue, and light portrait pink.

◀ **Step Seven** Next, add cool colors to the zombie and begin building up the dark values. At this point, just experiment with the cools against the warms and have fun with the possibilities. Incorporating a bit of the green mixture from Step Four will help to harmonize the zombie with the background.

▶ **Step Eight** In this step, focus on adding textures in the background and within sections of the zombie. Begin by airbrushing or applying thin washes over large areas with a little burnt umber and lamp black until it becomes semi-opaque. Then, use a toothbrush and spatter the painting with a very tiny amount of window cleaner; the ammonia will eat through some of the paint and create a unique mottling. By applying the layer of burnt umber and lamp black over the whole illustration, you'll find that you've tie the zombie in with the background.

◄ Step Nine After giving your airbrush a quick rinse, load it with cobalt blue and Mars black. Then, give the entire illustration a light spray, thus unifying the warms and cools. Take a wet cloth and gently remove some of the overspray. If you don't have an airbrush, apply thin washes over the painting instead. By doing this, the illustration achieves a depth of wonderful, complex layers that you couldn't achieve otherwise. Now, because the zombie is blending in with the background, use white to add rim light along the left edge of the face to separate the him from the background and create a sense of drama. In this case, note that you need a strong core shadow for the rim light to be effective.

▶ Step Ten Next, we'll begin the process of working in multiple layers, using cut-gesso (about 80% water and 20% gesso). Using a #00 brush, apply about 6 to 8 layers of the cut-gesso on the zombie, spraying workable fixative after every couple of layers to retain the transparency of the underlying colors while building up the lights at the same time. Once finished with the gesso layers, bring out a variety of colored pencils and start to draw back into the illustration.

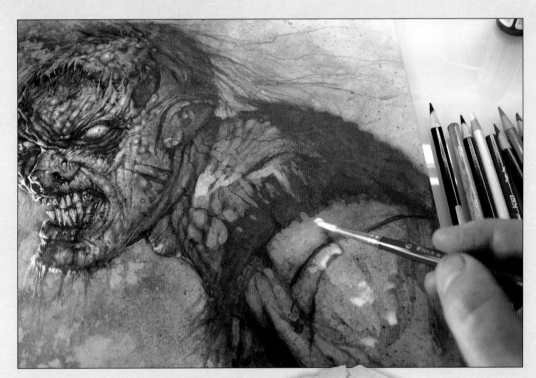

THE GORY DETAILS

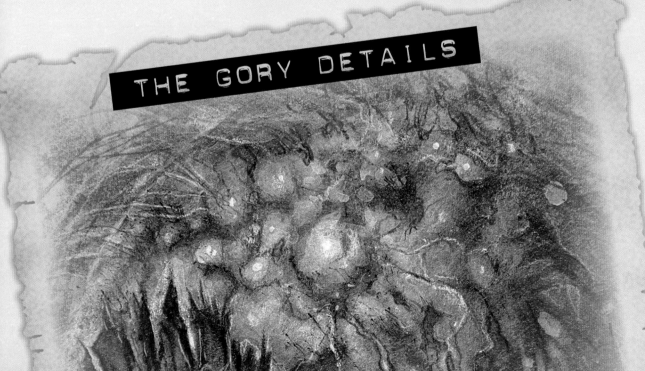

69

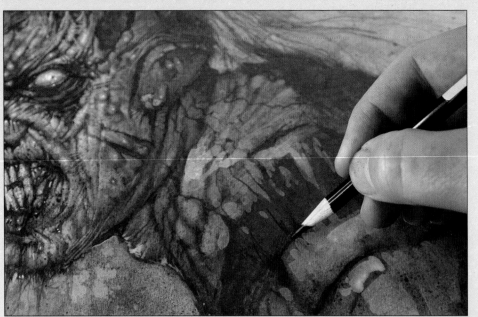

◄ **Step Eleven** Using a black colored pencil, detail the zombie by strengthening the darks, intensifying the shadows in the creases and around the boils. Constantly keep in mind the design of your shapes and lines; a drawing like this can easily become sloppy.

▶ **Step Twelve** For the final step, add another layer of wash, using some of the cut-gesso and mixing it with a little Hooker's green and lamp black to emphasize the look of rotting skin. Then draw back in with the black colored pencil, defining shapes, creating depth, and darkening any areas that get lost in all the washes. To add to the overall goriness of the piece, use a toothbrush to splatter pure naphthol red light over all the zombie's wounds for the look of fresh blood — the gruesome end to a fine illustration.

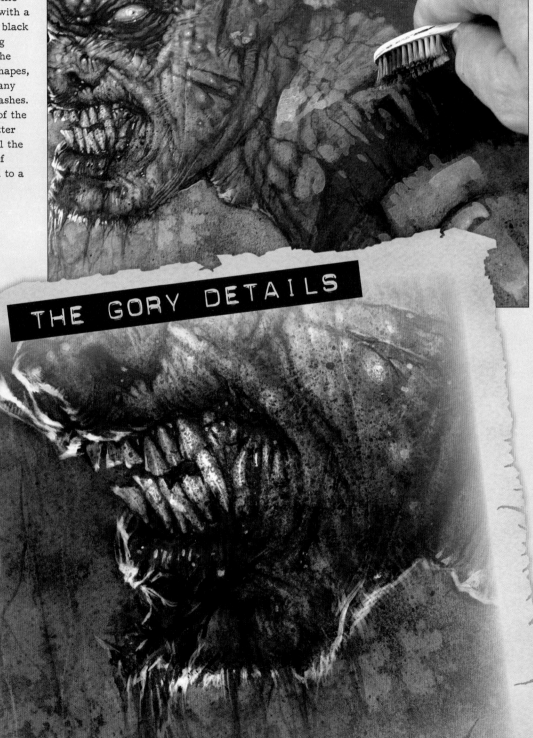

THE GORY DETAILS

71

Zombie Goth Girl

Sporting tattoos, piercings, and dramatic skin tones, this zombie Goth girl combines ethereal beauty with deadly intent. While she's not exactly the sort of girl you'd want to bring home to meet the parents, she's the perfect subject for another illustration in your growing portfolio of zombie monsters.

Materials
- Acrylic paints: Mars black, light portrait pink, cadmium red light, cadmium red deep hue, iridescent antique brown
- White cold pressed two-ply illustration board
- An assortment of colored pencils
- 600-grit sandpaper (any fine grain will do)
- Blowdryer
- Clear gesso
- House painting brush
- Assortment of small to medium acrylic paintbrushes
- Airbrush (optional)

▲ **Step One** Sketch out a dramatic composition, indicating the contrast of values and the flow of lines.

Step Two For this project, we will create a zombie Goth girl. Begin by working with a sharp black colored pencil on a white two-ply, cold-pressed illustration board. Crop tightly into her face and head, framing her deadly yet hauntingly beautiful face with locks of hair and wisps of smoke. (You can transfer this sketch; see "Transferring a Drawing" on page 25.)

72

Step Three Using a wide brush, quickly lay in broad strokes of diluted Mars black for the hair. For the face, mix a tiny bit of light portrait pink and cadmium red light with a substantial amount of water. Then use a big house painting brush to layer clear gesso over the drawing and underpainting, thus sealing it for the next step.

Step Four Once the gesso is dry, take the sandpaper and lightly stroke over the illustration. This creates a smooth surface for airbrushing and seals the drawing at the same time.

Step Five The eyes play an important part in the Gothic look. Take a little cadmium red deep hue mixed with a hint of light portrait pink, and then thin it out with water to paint the rims of her eyes. Next, outline the eyes with some Mars black and cadmium red deep hue to give them a graphic definition.

Step Six Taking a sharp black colored pencil, focus on the intricate design of her tattoos. Carefully design attractive shapes and alternate the lines from thick to thin, also paying attention to how they wrap around her bone structure. For the smoke, use a 30% cool gray colored pencil. Notice that the shapes in the smoke are carefully designed as well.

Step Seven Two other striking and recognizable Gothic features are pale skin combined with dark hair. Make a mixture of about 20% white gesso and 80% water. Then, using a medium-sized brush, begin to paint thin layers over the face. This process requires about five or six layers, so you can use a blowdryer after each layer to speed up the process. Next, darken the hair considerably by painting it with a couple of coats of diluted Mars black. For the lips and brow bone, you can use some iridescent antique brown and cadmium red deep hue for a bloody, coppery look.

▶ **Step Eight** Going back to the eyes, take a pink colored pencil and start softening the red, giving it a more realistic look. Next, use the same pencil to lightly shade in the tip of the nose, portions of the forehead, and beneath the eye to hint at the life that was once there. With a gray pencil, add some nose and lip piercings as her accessories of choice. Then focus on the tattoos, using a white colored pencil to outline them. This creates a slight 3-dimensional quality and also ties the tattoos into the smoke.

▼ **Step Nine** Next, use the airbrush to begin softening and darkening some areas. Fill the airbrush with the paint colors of the area that you are working on at that moment. Soften the edges around the face, the eyes, and the smoke. Then, darken the hair a bit. If you don't have an airbrush, build up thin layers of paint to darken or soften areas.

Step Ten For the final step, add any highlights to areas that need to pop, including the eyes, the piercings, and even the teeth.

Zombie Voodoo Doll

Even tiny things can be deadly in the world of zombies, as seen in this voodoo doll. Boasting life-draining needles and flame-inspired patterns, this illustration focuses on the supernatural elements that have become part of the zombie legend.

Materials
- Acrylic paints: Viridian hue permanent, turquoise deep, cadmium red light, iridescent antique brown, Turner's yellow
- #2 pencil
- Two-ply cold-pressed white illustration board (7" x 15")
- An assortment of colored pencils
- White gesso
- Old toothbrush
- Acrylic paint palette
- Variety of small acrylic brushes

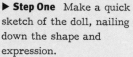 ▶ **Step One** Make a quick sketch of the doll, nailing down the shape and expression.

Step Two For the zombie voodoo doll painting, we'll begin with a white illustration board and a regular #2 pencil. This board will give a "toothy" texture, while the #2 pencil enables us to smudge the lines and achieve a dirty look. In contrast, vellum paper (which we used for many of the other projects in this book) produces a creamy texture and allows the artist to achieve clean and precise lines. This choice is just a matter of preference. (You can transfer this sketch; see "Transferring a Drawing" on page 25.)

Step Three Block in the doll, then start working on the dress details. The smudging and grittiness of the pencil actually contributes to the look of this subject.

Step Four Then add some flame-inspired patterns and exotic designs on the dress. Once the dark accents and life-draining needles are in place, we are ready for the colors.

NOT A RELIGION

Not considered a religion, voodoo doesn't have the structure usually associated with other faiths: No regular meetings or official priests. Today, variations of this belief system are found in Brazil, Cuba, Puerto Rico, the Caribbean, and West Africa. In the United States, voodoo is commonly practiced in New Orleans, the western Louisiana bayou, and areas of South Carolina. Each of these areas has a slightly different variation from Candomblé to Umbanda, from Arará to Shango, from Santeria to Lukumi.

79

◄ **Step Five** Begin with very diluted washes of acrylic paint, sticking with earth tones such as iridescent antique brown and viridian hue permanent. Painting inside the lines isn't a big concern on this illustration.

▼ **Step Six** Using a little bit of cadmium red light and a lot of water, put a warm wash over the face and body. Then, use some cool turquoise deep as accents to give a striking contrast to the red tones. Next, take an old toothbrush, dip it into the already mixed paints on your palette and spatter it all over the illustration.

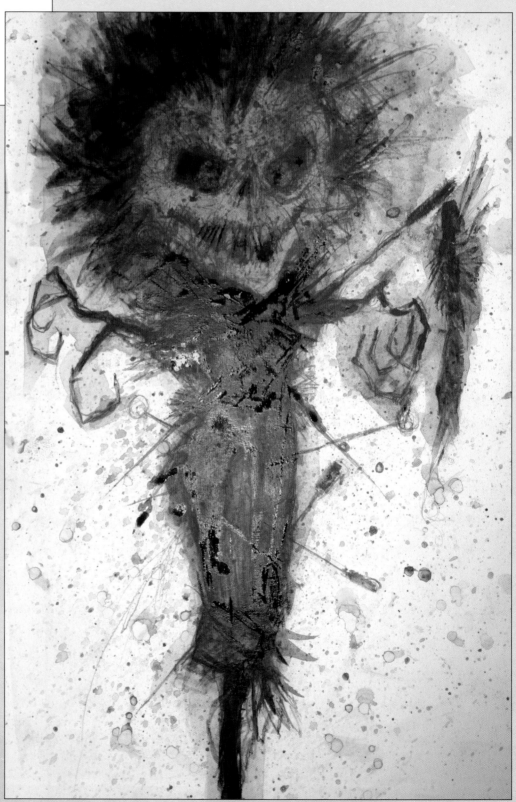

Step Seven In this step, we'll concentrate on the zombie voodoo doll's face. To create a creepy, pasty look, mix a small amount of heavily diluted white gesso (about 60% water and 40% gesso). Then, with a small paintbrush, start laying in all the forms of the face, leaving the underpainting free of paint to suggest the wrinkles and creases.

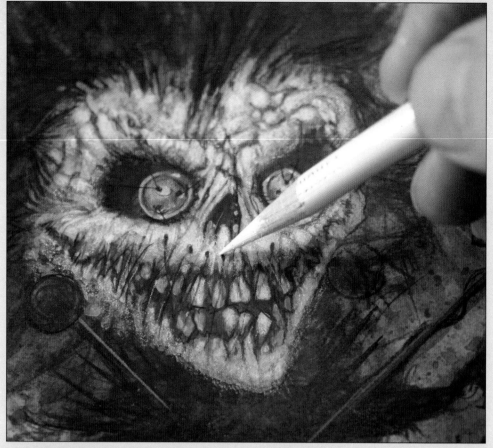

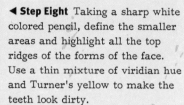

◄ **Step Eight** Taking a sharp white colored pencil, define the smaller areas and highlight all the top ridges of the forms of the face. Use a thin mixture of viridian hue and Turner's yellow to make the teeth look dirty.

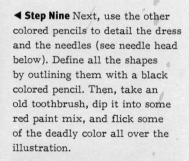

◄ **Step Nine** Next, use the other colored pencils to detail the dress and the needles (see needle head below). Define all the shapes by outlining them with a black colored pencil. Then, take an old toothbrush, dip it into some red paint mix, and flick some of the deadly color all over the illustration.

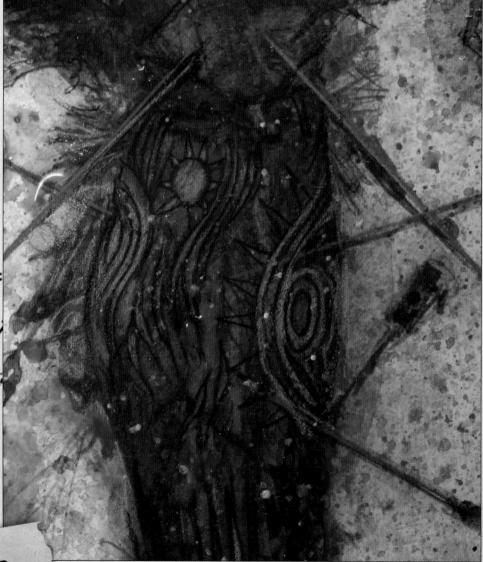

Zombie Pet

Unlike humans, zombies don't have to worry about their pets getting sick. Although this zombie cat might not purr or want to cuddle on your lap, it's built to last forever. This is one stray kitty you probably shouldn't let in the house on a rainy night.

Materials

- Acrylic paints: Mars black, Payne's gray, viridian hue permanent, turquoise deep, cerulean blue hue, cadmium red light, cadmium red deep hue, iridescent antique brown, unbleached titanium, phthalocyanine blue, Turner's yellow, light portrait pink
- Multimedia vellum paper
- An assortment of colored pencils
- 9" x 12" Masonite board
- White gesso
- Matte medium
- Workable spray fixative
- House painting brush
- Old toothbrush
- Acrylic paint palette
- Variety of small acrylic brushes
- Blowdryer

▲ **Step One** For this project, we will create our own zombie pet. With a finely sharpened black colored pencil, sketch the animal on vellum paper. Shade the dark values of the head first to quickly establish the maniacal personality of this house pet. (You can transfer this sketch; see "Transferring a Drawing" on page 25.)

Step Two Lay in the rest of the values on the head, and follow with the body. I added some thumbnails along the edge of the paper. I decided to leave them there to test different color schemes and also because they contributed to the overall charm of the picture.

◄ Step Three Next, we'll make the zombie pet look extremely emaciated and ratty. To achieve this, first, pull his mouth back to reveal long, grotesque teeth; then draw long swift lines that wrap around his skeletal body; and finally, add some unsightly growths on his head and rib cage. Use broken lines on his ears and legs to show the wear and tear of his skin.

▼ Step Four Once the drawing is done, make a color copy, and select the sepia tone setting. Then take the copy, spray it with workable spray fixative, and soak it in some water. After placing the wet picture on a Masonite board, mix a solution of 50% water and 50% matte medium in a bowl. Then use a big house brush to slather this mixture over the drawing. This mounts the picture on the board and provides a sturdy surface that won't warp when we start painting with watered-down acrylics.

Step Five Once the board is dry, use an extremely watered-down mixture of cerulean blue and Mars black to lay in the skin tone of the zombie cat, giving it a corpse-like feel. Then paint the mouth, the eyes, and the gashes with a thicker mixture of cadmium red light and cadmium red deep hue to create a deadly effect.

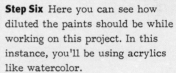

Step Six Here you can see how diluted the paints should be while working on this project. In this instance, you'll be using acrylics like watercolor.

Step Seven Dilute Payne's gray and then layer the drawing with this wash several times to bring the warm reds and cool blues, together. Then, take a blowdryer and quickly dry the painting. Next, start adding a thin color of Turner's yellow and viridian hue on certain parts of the creature's body and teeth to emphasize its jaundice and unhygienic qualities.

Step Eight Take an old toothbrush and dip it into a mixture of cadmium red deep and cadmium red light. Then flick it to create gruesome blood all around the mouth. After washing the toothbrush, dip it into a diluted mixture of Payne's gray and phthalocyanine blue, and then splatter it all over the picture, giving it a dirty, vintage look. Note: I experimented with the thumbnails on the side to come up with ideas for the painting.

Step Nine Using your color pencils, begin to delineate the features of the animal's face. With a warm gray pencil, accentuate the stringy texture of the creature's skin and also bring out the highlights. Next, using a black colored pencil, darken all the shadows and orifices. Then use a variety of other warm and cool pencils to deepen the colors of the acrylic washes.

ZOMBIE
CAT

DETAILS

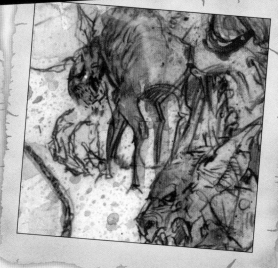

Midnight Snack

For centuries, vampires have been having all the fun. Who says that zombies can't be sensuous and romantic too? This illustration boasts a simple diagonal composition and tight cropping. Both elements add to the intimacy of this zombie with a discerning appetite, out for a night on the town.

Materials

- Acrylic paints: Mars black, viridian hue permanent, Hooker's green, cadmium red deep hue, portrait pink, Turner's yellow, iridescent brown, titanium white, cadmium yellow
- Small acrylic paintbrush
- Vellum paper
- Masonite board
- Matte medium
- House painting brush
- Old toothbrush
- Palette
- Computer system and Photoshop®
- Scanner

Step One Create a thumbnail drawing of the scene, indicating the main shapes and blocking in the basic values.

▶ **Step Two** Using a red colored pencil, block in the drawing on a piece of vellum paper. (You can transfer this sketch; see "Transferring a Drawing" on page 25.) Creating a close-up of the two main characters and exposing the woman's neck will create a great sense of vulnerability for the viewer and a certain amount of sadistic sensuality. Once the drawing is complete, make a copy of it and spray it with workable spray fixative. First, soak it in water for a couple of seconds; then mount it on a masonite board with a mixture of 50% matte medium and 50% water, using an old house painting brush. These steps offer several benefits: one, you'll have a flat, undistorted surface; two, you'll have a great texture to draw on; and three, you won't have to worry about scanning a warped illustration board in the final stages. Next, mix a little bit of viridian hue permanent with a lot of water and, using a big brush, quickly cover the zombie with this wash.

▶ Step Three Then, use an airbrush to lay in all the shadows and core shadows on the zombie's face. If you don't have an airbrush, stroke in the shadows using thin washes of paint instead. For the color, mix a little viridian hue permanent and Mars black. Also, softly and subtly go over the girl's face with the green mixture to establish a cohesive piece. To create the unsightly boils on his face, add little green circles. Then, take a small paintbrush and highlight the center of each one with a bit of white gesso and water.

▼ Step Four To add more texture to the zombie's skin, take an old toothbrush and dip it into the colors on the palette. Then, flick the paint onto the creature. Note: You may have noticed from the other illustrations in the book that the old toothbrush is a reliable tool of mine.

◄ Step Five For the girl's skin tone, use a mixture of cadmium red deep hue and portrait pink. The colors of the zombie should complement the color of the girl: He should be a ghoulish green and she should be a warm, glowing red.

► Step Six Airbrush the rest of the girl's face and neck with a little Turner's yellow and iridescent antique brown. For the core shadows, mix in a tiny bit of Hooker's green. If you don't have an airbrush, build up thin layers of paint, creating soft blends to suggest the curvature of her forms.

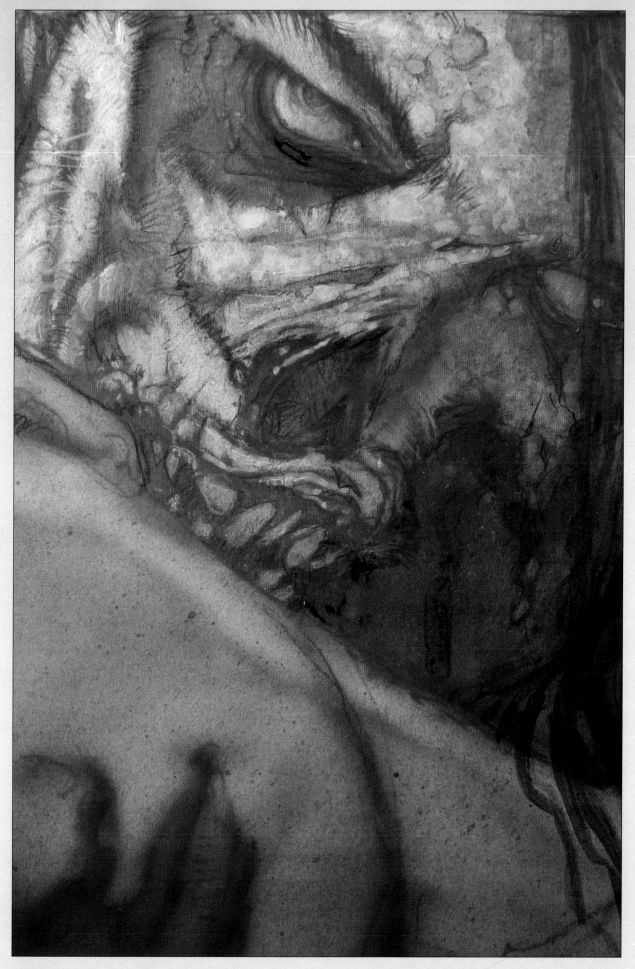

Step Seven Now, begin to bring out some of the hot spots on the zombie's face to explain the light source. Use a white colored pencil for this, making sure to design your strokes as you shade. To create a milky texture for his eyes, mix a little portrait pink and titanium white.

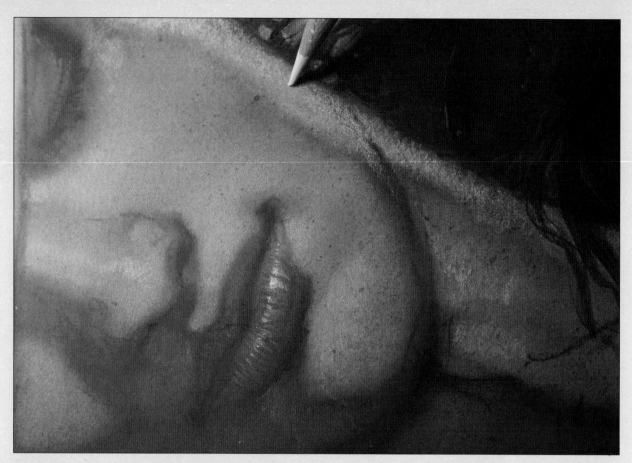

Step Eight Next, return to the girl. We want to portray the warm, peaceful life that pulsates inside her, thus creating a contrast with our dead zombie. Do this by imagining that her light source comes from a nearby crackling fireplace. To achieve this glow, fill the airbrush with half cadmium yellow and half water. Then, spray a light mist over her face and neck. If you don't have an airbrush, apply a thin layer of the wash instead. Next, take a warm yellow colored pencil and highlight certain areas of her face and neck, at the same time adding some texture over the smooth layers of paint.

Step Nine We are now done with the painting aspect. To enhance the painting with a few digital adjustments, follow the remaining steps. Begin by scanning it into Photoshop®. For this piece, we will be working directly on a Wacom Tablet (a graphic or digital pen).

Step Ten By using Photoshop® on the very last stage of the illustration, you can achieve a wonderful, eye-popping finish in just a matter of minutes. Select the burnish tool and start picking out hot spots on various areas of the highlights.

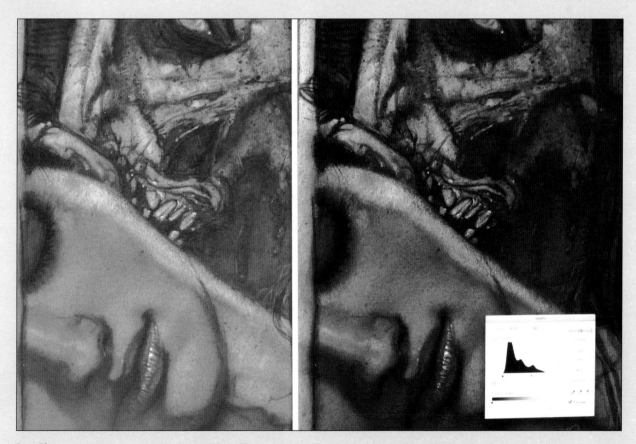

Step Eleven Here we see a split-screen view. The image on the right can be achieved by using the levels tool in Photoshop® to saturate the values. Using levels can make certain areas—or the whole picture—darker or lighter. (See page 101.)

▶ **Step Twelve** Next, select the paintbrush tool. Set it at a large diameter of about 45 pixels and at a minimum hardness. Bring some warm yellow lighting onto the zombie's face. Choose a 3% yellow from the color swatch and, using the paintbrush, lightly go over his face until you're satisfied with the effect. Then, select a turquoise blue. Using the same brush tool (adjusting the diameter of the circle accordingly), go over the side of the zombie's face and the rim lighting on the girl, with a saturation of about 2 or 3%. Next, select an orange color for the rest of the girl's skin tone. Then, lightly dust her face and neck with a saturation of about 5%. This will emphasize the complementary colors of the image.

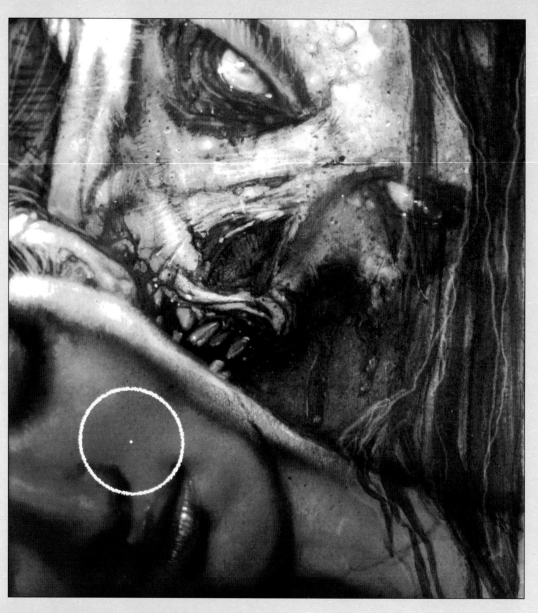

◀ **Step Thirteen** When using the computer, be conscious of avoiding a slick "computer generated" look. One way to do this is by adding interesting textures. Select the smudge tool and decrease it to the size 3 pixels and keep the hardness at 100%. Then, go over the zombie's cheekbones, nose, and eyebrows for a more traditional and illustrative effect. Zombie eyes — or the lack of them — are integral to a walking-dead character. In this case, use the blur tool and go over the whites of the zombie's eyes to create a murky look. Then, select the smudge tool and, with a small diameter, add strange, alien-looking highlights.

▶ **Step Fourteen** For the final step, we want to tie in the warm colors of the girl's face with the cool colors of the zombie. Select the paintbrush tool and set it to about 25 pixels. Then, choose the turquoise blue again and lightly brush the light areas of her face and neck. If you want the hungry zombie to be the center of attention — like it is in this illustration — use the levels tool to bring down the value of your sleeping beauty.

97

Digital Illustration Materials

Digital illustration can result in highly detailed, fiercely dynamic artwork. Unlike drawing or painting, digital illustration allows you to make dramatic enhancements with just a few clicks of a button. Before working on the projects in this chapter, note that it's important to have an understanding of the basic tools and functions of your image-editing software (I prefer Photoshop®). However, if you don't have a background in digital illustration, you can still use these projects as references for drawing or painting—each piece of art begins with a drawing or painting by hand.

Paintbrushes

Acrylic Paints

Colored Pencils

Paint Palette

Materials Checklist

To complete all the illustration projects in this book, you'll need to purchase the materials below. Note that the exact materials needed for each project are listed at the start of each project:

• Acrylic paints: Mars black, Payne's gray, viridian hue permanent, turquoise deep, cerulean blue hue, cadmium red light, iridescent antique brown, titanium white, cadmium red deep hue, Turner's yellow, cadmium yellow
• Acrylic paint palette
• Palette box
• Variety of small acrylic brushes
• Inexpensive house painting brush
• An assortment of colored pencils (30% cool gray and black)
• Tracing paper
• Masonite board (8" x 10")
• Vellum paper
• Workable spray fixative
• Matte medium
• Airbrush (optional)
• Computer system and Photoshop®
• Scanner

Computer System

To embark on your journey in digital illustration, you'll need a computer system, a scanner, and image-editing software. In the setup at left, you'll see that you can configure multiple monitors for one computer system. This can help you spread out your work; you can bleed the monitors so that your image crosses over onto multiple screens, allowing you to see much more of the image at once. You can also use the multiple monitors to hold various control panels, so you aren't constantly minimizing windows to create room on the screen. Although it's ideal to work with several monitors, all you really need is one.

Image-Editing Software

There is a variety of image-editing software available, but many would agree that Adobe® Photoshop® is the most widely used. Below are short summaries of some basic functions used in the projects throughout this book.

Photoshop Basics

Image Resolution: When scanning your drawing or painting into Photoshop, it's important to scan it at 300 dpi (dots per inch) and 100% the size of the original. A higher dpi carries more pixel information and determines the quality at which your image will print. However, If you intend for the image to be a piece of digital art only, you can set the dpi as low as 72. View the dpi and size under the menu Image › Image Size.

Eraser Tool: The eraser tool is found in the basic tool bar. When working on a background layer, the tool removes pixels to reveal a white background. You can adjust the diameter and opacity of the brush to control the width and strength of the eraser.

Dodge and Burn Tools: The dodge and burn tools, terms borrowed from the old dark room, are also found on the basic tool bar. *Dodge* is synonymous with *lighten,* and *burn* is synonymous with *darken.* On the settings bar under "range," you can select highlights, midtones, or shadows. Select which of the three you'd like to dodge or burn, and the tool will only affect these areas. Adjust the width and exposure (or strength) as desired.

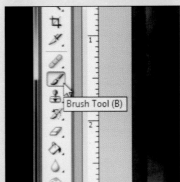

Paintbrush Tool: The paintbrush tool, on the basic tool bar in Photoshop, allows you to apply layers of color to your canvas. Like the eraser, dodge, and burn tools, you can adjust the diameter and opacity of the brush to control the width and strength of your strokes.

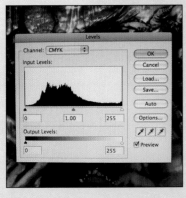

Levels: With this tool (under the menu Image › Adjustments), you can change the brightness, contrast, and range of values within an image. The black, midtone, and white of the image are represented by the three markers along the bottom of the graph. Slide these markers horizontally. Moving the black marker right will darken the overall image, moving the white marker left will lighten the overall image, and sliding the midtone marker left or right will bring the midtones darker or lighter, respectively.

Color Picker: Choose the color of your "paint" in the color picker window. Select your hue by clicking within the vertical color bar; then move the circular cursor around the box to change the color's tone.

101

Zombie Romance

Everybody needs a dose of romantic literature once in a while, even the undead. So, for this illustration we'll be creating a zombie romance book cover. Who said romance was dead?

Materials
- Acrylic paints: Cadmium yellow, cadmium red light, viridian hue permanent, cerulean blue hue, Mars black, Turner's yellow
- House painting brush
- Small acrylic paintbrushes
- Palette
- Tracing paper
- Masonite board
- Workable spray fixative
- Matte medium
- Assortment of colored pencils
- Airbrush (optional)
- Computer system and Photoshop®
- Scanner

▲ **Step One** Following the thumbnail drawing (above), create a sketch using a red colored pencil on tracing paper. (You can transfer this sketch; see "Transferring a Drawing" on page 25.) After blocking in the drawing, make a photocopy of it. Spray the photocopy with workable spray fixative, then soak it in water for a couple of seconds. Next, mount it onto a masonite board by laying it on the board and brushing it with a mixture of 50% matte medium and 50% water.

▲ **Step Two** Once that dries, start laying in some colors using a medium-sized acrylic brush. For the flames, use a mixture of cadmium yellow and cadmium red light combined with a good deal of water. For the zombies, use a very watered down combination of viridian hue permanent and cerulean blue hue.

◀ **Step Three** With the airbrush, quickly lay in the shadows, core shadows, as well as more colors for the skin tone. Then, spray some Turner's yellow on the male zombie's chest to reflect the colors of the flames. Soften the hair and feather out the edges, similar to the technique used on the flames — this will create a dramatic effect. If you don't have an airbrush, build up thin washes of paint, blending the edges for a soft look.

Step Four Next, switch to the colored pencils and start to draw back into the illustration. With a black colored pencil, add dark accents to the eye sockets, nose, and corners of the mouth.

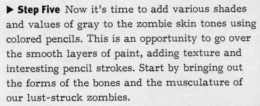

▶ **Step Five** Now it's time to add various shades and values of gray to the zombie skin tones using colored pencils. This is an opportunity to go over the smooth layers of paint, adding texture and interesting pencil strokes. Start by bringing out the forms of the bones and the musculature of our lust-struck zombies.

◀ **Step Six** Still using the colored pencils, add some fun make-up to our femme fatal. Then, bring out more highlights on the male. Make sure to keep his features chiseled and handsome.

103

Step Seven Add some holes all over the zombies' forms to emphasize the brittle nature of their skeletal bodies. Do this by painting in some shapes with crisp edges, using watered down Mars black. To add depth to these holes, go back in with the black colored pencil and darken the center of the shapes.

Step Eight To increase the intensity of the image, go back in with a paintbrush and add some cadmium red light and Turner's yellow to the fire. Keep your brush strokes splotchy, but make sure they blow in one direction. Then, using diluted cadmium red light and Turner's yellow, spatter some fine drops of paint over the zombies for texture. Now that the illustration is 90% done, scan it into your computer. In Photoshop®, you can quickly and effectively add some eye-popping details and play around with special effects.

Step Nine First experiment with the flames around the two lovers. Then, select the paintbrush tool and go into its options bar. Decrease the diameter of the brush, bring the hardness level way down, and chose a light yellow from the color palette. By doing this, the lovebirds are brought even closer to the foreground.

Step Ten A bright blazing fire would make an excellent backdrop for our zombie lovers. So, increase your brush size and opacity; then choose a warm, bright yellow from your palette. Keep the outer edges of the flames orange to maintain realism. Note that it's still important to remain conscious of the design of your shapes and strokes, even when working on the computer. Then outline the zombies with a hot orange-red to make them vibrate.

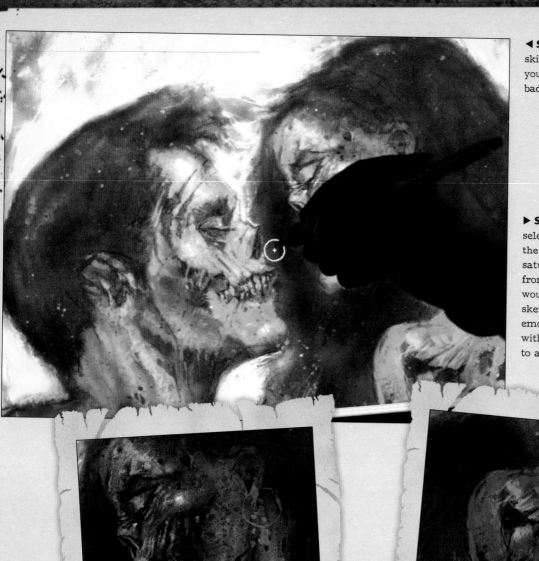

◄ **Step Eleven** Add more yellow to their skin and teeth. When you're a zombie, you don't worry about little things like bad breath or hygiene.

► **Step Twelve** For the final step, select the levels option and darken the two characters. This increases the saturation of color and separates them from the flames. This painting is what would be used as a color production sketch or color comp. It conveys the emotions of the characters and story without having to be taken all the way to a finished illustration.

Face The female's red lipstick looks like blood, so to make her as gruesome as possible — and to create a fun play on how lipstick smears during a lusty smooch — use your paintbrush tool and select a fiery shade of red. Make sure that the "hardness" of the tool is soft, then start painting around her mouth. After this, increase the hardness of the brush and the opacity as well, then add some gory blood splatter on her cheeks.

Shoulder Even though our female zombie is showing a lot of skin, she's made almost entirely out of bones. To play up the reflective nature of the bony surface, add some highlights around the edges of the fractured holes.

Hand Most artists think that drawing a hand is both difficult and time-consuming, but all you need are the correct number of fingers and a little indication form. The viewer's eye will accept this because most of the time, we see hands in our peripheral vision — not as the main focus. Still using your paintbrush tool, select a darker red and paint around the fingertips. Then, choose a deep cherry red and increase the opacity. Paint deep holes within the lighter red to show the depth of the wounds she is inflicting on her lover.

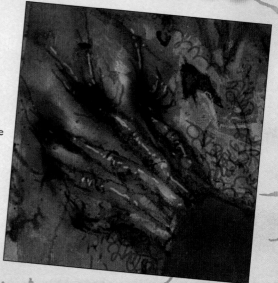

107

Voodoo Queen

For this project we will be creating what's known as a color concept sketch or production sketch, not a finished illustration. This type of comp is used to give a director or producer an idea of character design and environment.

Materials
- Acrylic paints: Mars black, Payne's gray, viridian hue permanent, turquoise deep, cerulean blue hue, cadmium red light, iridescent antique brown, titanium white, cadmium red deep hue, Turner's yellow
- House painting brush
- Palette
- Variety of small acrylic brushes
- Tracing paper (7" x 10")
- Masonite board (8" x 10")
- Workable spray fixative
- An assortment of colored pencils
- Matte medium
- Airbrush (optional)
- Computer system and Photoshop®
- Scanner

Step One To create a voodoo queen, start off with a sketch using red colored pencil over a piece of 7" x 10" tracing paper.

Step Two Now create a sketch of your thumbnail using red colored pencil over a piece of 7" x 10" tracing paper. (You can transfer this sketch; see "Transferring a Drawing" on page 25.) Once you're satisfied with the sketch, make a colored copy of it. Then, take the copy outside and spray it with workable spray fixative. When that dries, wet mount it to a masonite board by taking a big house brush and brushing on a mixture of 50% water and 50% matte medium. This step is crucial because it will allow you to work on a flat, undistorted surface. Once the board is dry, start layering in colors: cool purples and blues for the background, and warmer tones for the voodoo queen. Make sure the colors are heavily diluted with water.

108

▲ Step Three After laying in your washes, bring out an airbrush to create a softer effect and to speed up the process of the initial lay-in stage. Take a little iridescent antique brown mixed with a bit of cadmium red deep hue and airbrush over the face and chest. If you don't have an airbrush, apply thin washes of paint, softly blending in the shadows to create form.

▲ Step Five For the highlights and crests of the folds on her robe, mix a little bit of titanium white with a good amount of water and lay it in with a small acrylic brush. This will create a nice contrast between the obvious strokes of the brush and the softness of the airbrush.

▲ Step Four Next, airbrush (or paint) the darker values found in the folds of her robe using combinations of Payne's gray, turquoise deep, cadmium red light, and viridian hue permanent. When you don't have a reference, the key to making these colors believable comes from using colors found in the background. Then, also, imagine what kind of light source is focused on the subject. In this case, we want her to be in a very warm light.

Step Six Use a variety of colored pencils to draw the queen's facial features and skin highlights, and to reinforce the design of the turban. Unlike zombies, our voodoo queen's skin is intact, so make sure to keep her features subtle and the colors pastel.

◄ **Step Seven** In this image, we want to communicate the power and magic she possesses, so start to give her exotic tattoos, ornate jewelry, and intricate designs on her robe.

▶ **Step Eight** Finish the tattoos across her face, and then start to deal with the light source. It should originate from a group of candles on the lower left-hand side of the illustration. Taking a small paintbrush, use some Turner's yellow and create graphic flame shapes. To soften these flames and to make them glow, airbrush over them with Turner's yellow or build up thin washes of paint.

◄ **Step Nine** Mix a little Turner's yellow and cadmium red light, and then use a small paintbrush to add this color to the candle flames. Using the same mixture, fill the airbrush and lightly mist the flames again (or apply thin layers of paint). Then, use these warm colors to brighten the turban and all the areas that would be hit by the candlelight. You can also add some extra mystical jewelry by quickly indicating shapes with a very small brush. Just hit these shapes with warm highlights to finish them off.

▲ **Step Ten** Darken the robe so it's closer to the value of the background. Use turquoise deep, cerulean blue hue, and a little Mars black. Lightly spray these colors over the fabric with the airbrush or build up thin washes of paint.

▶ **Step Eleven** Once you're finished with hand-painting the illustration, scan it into Photoshop. At this point, we'll start adding a demonic skull emerging from the wisps of candle smoke. Begin by defining shadow shapes found in a normal human skull. Then, take the brush tool and adjust the diameter to size. Pick a dark indigo color from the palette and start drawing in the shapes. We will not be using layers for this illustration.

Step Twelve Finish the rest of the skull in the same manner. Then, start adding dark shapes around the flames to convey the transparent characteristics of wafting smoke. All this is done using the same tool and color, just adjust the opacity, hardness, and size of the brush as you see fit.

Step Thirteen For a more ominous look, select levels and lower the values of the whole illustration considerably. Then, soften the edges around the voodoo queen by using the dodge tool. Change the range to shadow, keep the exposure low, and just go over her silhouette.

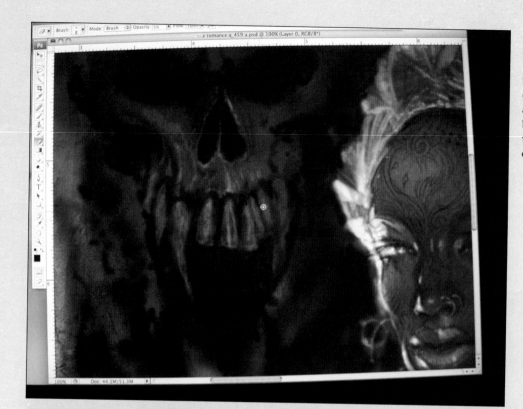

Step Fourteen In this step, the skull really comes alive. Select the dodge tool, adjust its diameter accordingly, then click highlight for the range and lower the exposure. Then, begin adding the highlights on the teeth, nasal cavity, and cheekbones.

◀ **Step Fifteen** To create the smoke that emanates from the skull, simply use the eraser tool set at about 7% opacity and 0% hardness for the outer edges.

▶ **Step Sixteen** Brighten up the highlights in her eyes, her turban, and the edges of her robe by selecting the paintbrush tool and picking a bright lemon yellow from the palette. Keep the brush hardness set at soft to maintain a glowing effect. Again, this illustration is considered a production sketch and is used merely to reflect the flavor of character and story. It does not need to be rendered to a tight finish.

Zombie Assassin

This illustration features a hired zombie killer, ready and willing to do the dirty work—for a price. For this piece, we will use Photoshop® to tint and enhance the illustration. This procedure works especially well when you're doing a production drawing or character design, and you need to create variations on mood or tone without taking too much time.

Materials
- Black colored pencil
- Vellum paper
- Scanner
- Computer system and Photoshop®

▶ **Step One** Start your drawing, using a sharp black colored pencil on vellum paper. While this type of paper is a bit expensive, it allows for a beautiful, creamy line quality. Work out all the details of the zombie's anatomy, designing the veins in a way that almost resembles tattoo art. The majority of the time on this project will be spent on the drawing itself. (You can transfer this sketch; see "Transferring a Drawing" on page 25.) When you're done with the full value drawing, scan it into Photoshop®.

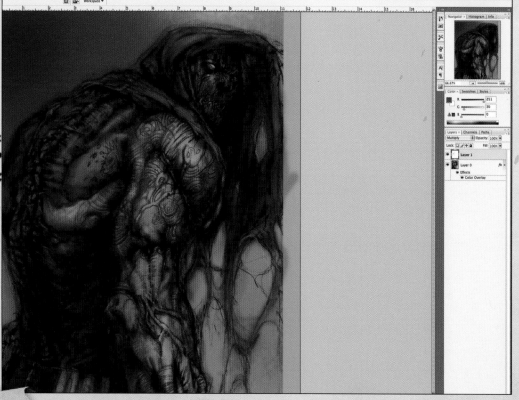

◀ **Step Two** Once you've scanned in your drawing, begin to experiment with the colors. Using the brush tool, adjust the diameter to size and lower the opacity so that you can layer your colors and value. For this to work, you'll need to change the mode in the brush options to "multiply." Begin with a shade of teal, then create a couple of layers so you can continue to experiment with colors if desired.

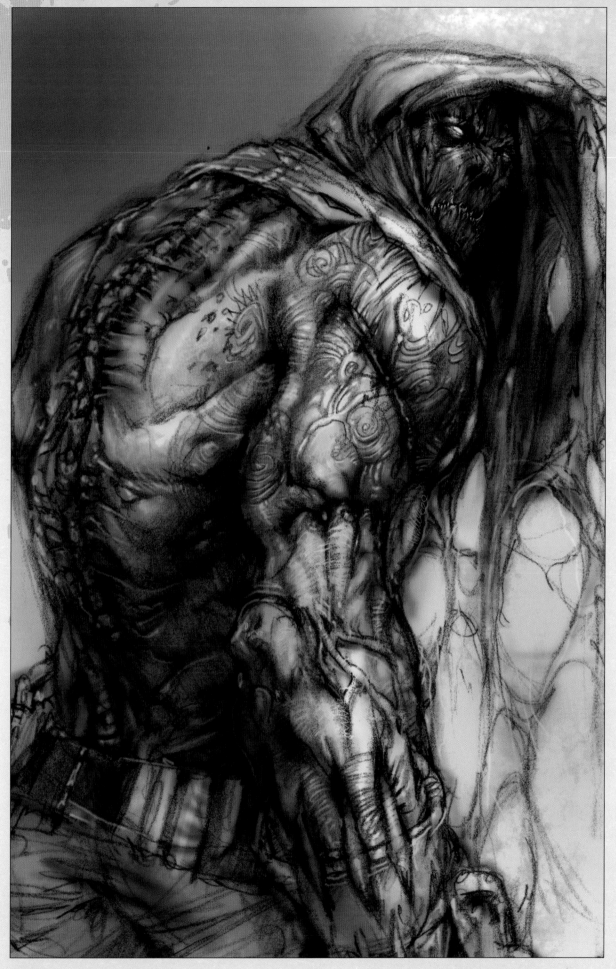

Step Three To complement the teal, select a warm gray with a tint of yellow and go over the whole image. Increase the brush size and decrease the hardness to about 10%. Also, bring down the opacity so that the color acts like a thin veil over the illustration. Then, warm up parts of his musculature to give the illustration a more organic feel.

Step Four For more saturation, select your levels and darken the whole image by about 10%. Next, select a magenta color that will harmonize with the teal, and add a bit of it to the zombie's tattered hood.

Step Five Once satisfied with your values and tone, move on to the highlights. Accent the dimensions of the zombie assassin's anatomy by selecting the eraser tool. Bring the opacity and hardness down to about 20% and adjust the diameter to size. Then, slowly lighten the centers of the forms.

Step Six Repeat the process used in Step Five for the zombie's eyes and face.

final art.psd @ 66.7% (RGB/8)

Step Seven Now, we'll make the veins more prominent by following them with a darker shadow underneath. Remember to keep the veins wrapped around the forms of his muscles to make them look believable. Soften the zombie ever so slightly by selecting the dodge tool and brightening the shoulder. Next, choose the blur tool and click the "lighten" mode. Keep the strength at about 50% and use it to go over the whole zombie.

◀ **Step Eight** Next, we'll add some unique markings to our undead assassin, creating designs that mimic bloody wounds. First, chose a bright red. Then, using the paintbrush, begin to draw some zigzag lines, making sure that they follow the zombie's anatomy. After this, give the lines a slight shadow by selecting a red that is a few values darker. Make his veins look like they are about to burst out of his skin by coloring them red as well.

◀ **Step Nine** Then, repeat the process in Step Eight. Add some tribal-esque designs to the zombie assassin's face and forehead.

▶ For the final touch, add the hint of a futuristic gadget to his belt, revealing that this zombie is both dangerous and technologically savvy. With a bright yellowish green, use the brush tool and keep the opacity and hardness set on high. Then, just stroke in a few quick shapes and add some reflected light to his elbow and forearm, weighting down the zombie and balancing the composition.

A ZOMBIE MOVIE FEST

To get in the spirit of things, consider hosting your own zombie movie fest. Invite a group of friends over for an evening or a weekend. The list below contains films that contributed to our modern day monster. Don't forget to provide snacks. You don't want your pals to end up brain dead and lethargic. Neighbors might mistake them for zombies.

White Zombie: 1932 by Edward and Victor Halperin
Ouanga: 1936 by George Terwilliger
Revolt of the Zombies: 1936 by Victor Halperin
I Walked with a Zombie: 1943 by Jacques Tourneur
The Last Man On Earth: 1964 by Sidney Salkow
Night of the Living Dead: 1968 by George Romero
The Return of the Living Dead: 1985 by Dan O'Bannon
Dawn of the Dead: 1978 by George Romero
Day of the Dead: 1985 by George Romero
Braindead: 1992 by Peter Jackson
Dellamorte Dellamore: 1994 by Michele Soavi
Land of the Dead: 2005 by George Romero
Shaun of the Dead: 2004 by Edgar Wright
Dead Set: 2008 by Yann Demange

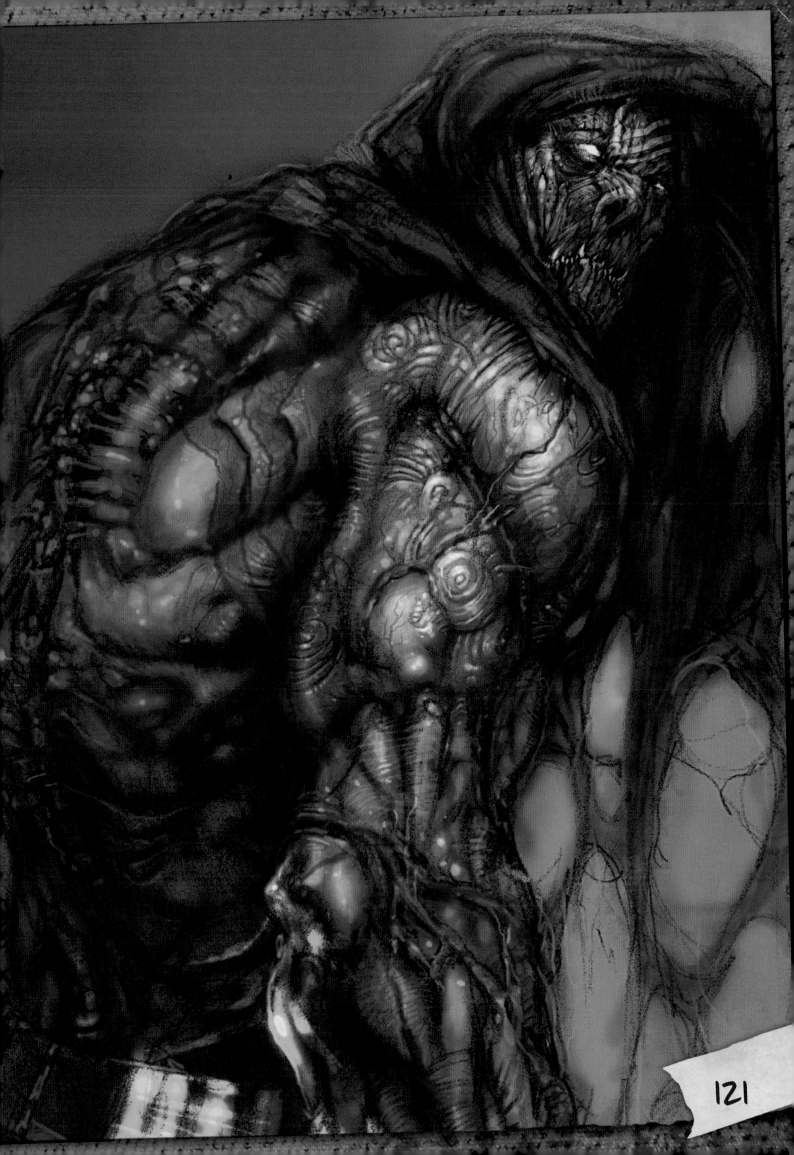

Great Zombie Apocalypse

Ever since the book *I Am Legend* came out in 1954, nearly every zombie movie has included some form of zombie apocalypse. From the 1968 film, *Night of the Living Dead*, to the 2009 flick, *Zombieland*, the landscape of the world is seen ravaged by these wandering, insatiable undead monsters—made even scarier by the fact that many of them used to be the protagonist's best friends.

Materials
- 30% cool gray colored pencil
- Black colored pencil
- Vellum paper
- Computer system and Photoshop®
- Scanner

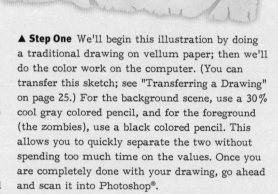

◀ **Step Two** First, create a layer for the background, and then select a cool color for the evening sky. Using the brush tool, select the multiply mode and adjust the master diameter and opacity accordingly. At this point, we are still experimenting with the color scheme, so keep the opacity light, and slowly build up the values.

▲ **Step One** We'll begin this illustration by doing a traditional drawing on vellum paper; then we'll do the color work on the computer. (You can transfer this sketch; see "Transferring a Drawing" on page 25.) For the background scene, use a 30% cool gray colored pencil, and for the foreground (the zombies), use a black colored pencil. This allows you to quickly separate the two without spending too much time on the values. Once you are completely done with your drawing, go ahead and scan it into Photoshop®.

▶ **Step Three** Now that there is some color in the background, you have something to play off and start to work on the front zombie. Create a new layer. With the brush tool, select a cool, sickly beige for the skin tone. For the fingers and ears, choose a warmer color to add a little realism.

Step Four Now for the gory part. From the color palette, select a red for the blood. Then, using the brush tool, outline the zombies' features and add blood splatter to the teeth, lips, and chin. Separate certain areas of the zombies into different layers so you can easily make changes and additions as the painting progresses.

▶ **Step Five** Use a different color scheme for the skin on the shorter zombie. Keep the opacity of the brush tool set on low, as if you are laying in a color wash using real paints.

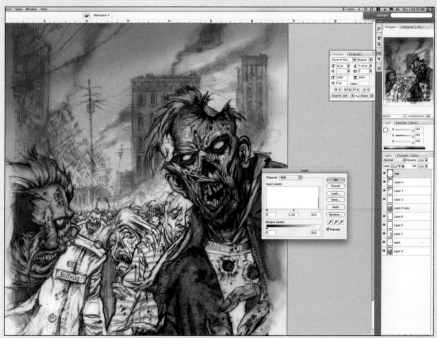

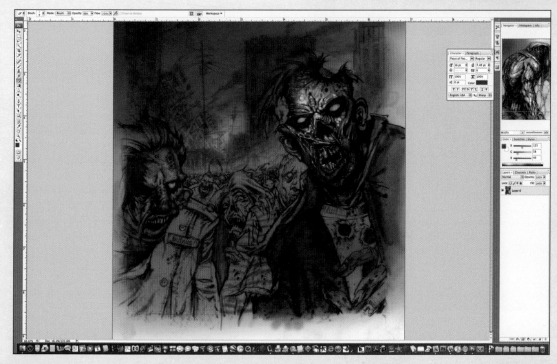

Step Six Now we're going to darken the whole image. Create a new layer and select an olive green from the color swatches. Again, keep the opacity low and increase the brush size. Keep the mode at multiply so the layers of color beneath will show through. This gives the image a grittier effect.

▲ **Step Seven** Now that the atmosphere is closer to what we want, we can go back to the leading zombie. Add more details by simply choosing the eraser tool — keep the opacity at about 20%. Pick out some highlights along the side of his mouth, forehead, teeth, and cheeks.

▲ **Step Eight** Next we'll work on the smaller zombie. Select the paintbrush tool and add a light layer of blue all over his face. Then, with the eraser tool, pick out some highlights to give more dimension to the forms. Also, use the eraser tool to draw back into his face, adding more texture. As for the hair, lay in a darker value for the big shape and then, using the brush tool, decrease the diameter and add some wispy strands. This zombie might have skin problems, but he takes pride in his full head of hair.

◄ **Step Nine** For the smaller zombie's shirt, select grayish white and use the brush tool to paint it in, leaving the folds and creases alone to allow the original drawing to show. Then, for texture, add some cross hatching by using the eraser tool.

◄ **Step Ten** Next, we'll focus on the chaotic background scene. Brighten up certain areas to set the stage for multiple fires. Do this by selecting the dodge tool and choose the highlight mode. For the smoky effect, keep the exposure at about 30%. Once this is done, go back in with the paintbrush tool and add some hot spots by choosing a cool yellow.

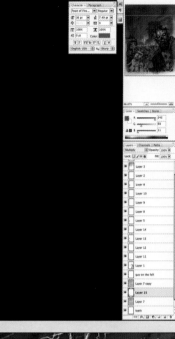

◄ Step Eleven Then, add thick dark clouds of smoke by using the paintbrush tool and keeping the hardness really low. Remember, in order to create realistic smoke, you must show that it has dimensions. Add some fire in the windows. Then, highlight the telephone lines and the falling building by using a very fine tip for the brush tool. The key to making the architecture believable is to keep the lines straight and thin and the perspective accurate.

◄ Step Twelve Now we're going to take it a step further and add lightning into the mix. Using the dodge tool, adjust the diameter and increase the hardness. Then, change the range to "highlights" and bring up the exposure to almost 100%. Draw shapes similar to old, gnarled tree branches. Once finished, select the paintbrush tool and add some highlights on the lightning with a light, turquoise blue.

► Step Thirteen You won't need a lot of details for the zombie crowd since the two main zombies in front are so flushed out. Just lay in some color for the background characters using the brush tool.

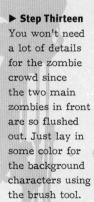

125

Step Fourteen With the brush tool, quickly indicate the zombie faces in the background. Then, select the eraser tool, set the opacity at about 15%, and tatter up the jacket of the main zombie. Also, add some threadbare and frayed texture to the profile of the zombie behind him.

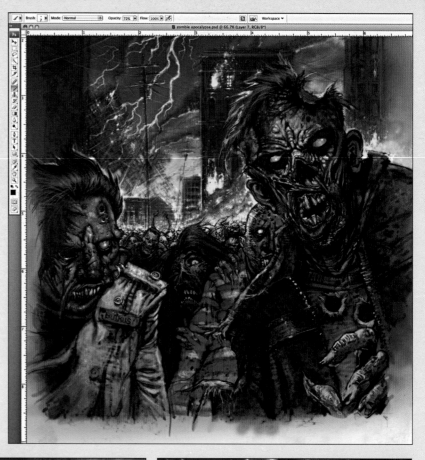

▼ **Step Fifteen** We're going to return to the main zombie next, adding into him some of the colors found in his friends and the environment. By doing this, we tie everything together and make the painting more cohesive. Also, add some more highlights to his face and hand.

▲ **Step Sixteen** You never know where or how you'll find inspiration. My six-year-old daughter gave me a brilliant idea — that the main zombie's head could catch on fire. To follow her advice, select the brush tool and increase the opacity for the color of the flames. Then, select the burn tool and add a shadow under and behind the flame. To make the flames look like they shoot away from his head, select the smudge tool, decrease the strength to about 20% and go over the area a couple of times.

127

The Nightmare Ends

Congratulations! You survived your first journey into the Fantasy Underground. In this book, you learned how to draw a wide variety of zombies, from a teenage zombie killer to a zombie Goth girl to a zombie assassin. You also experimented with black-and-white illustrations, acrylic paintings, and computer manipulation. The secrets of drawing the undead have been revealed, and as they say in the Underground: If you can capture the beast on paper, then you can control it. So, if you have successfully navigated through these projects you yourself, are now a Master of the Undead. May you continue to dominate zombies, near and far, until your next journey into the Fantasy Underground.

Meet the Authors

Mike Butkus

Mike Butkus, one of the top entertainment illustrators
and conceptual artists since 1990, has been involved in the
advertising, production, art direction, character development
and set design for more than 2,500 film and television series.
During the last ten years, Mike has been able to unleash his
twisted imagination on the rising gaming industry, designing and
illustrating fantastic creatures, characters, and environments for
all the interactive players to enjoy. To see Mike's own personal
work, which is now available for merchandising and licensing,
visit www.offleashconceptart.com or www.mikebutkus.net.

Merrie Destefano

Merrie Destefano left a 9-to-5 desk job to become a full-time
freelance editor and novelist, writing science fiction and fantasy.
With 20 years' experience in publishing, her background ranges
from award-winning graphic designer and illustrator to editor
of *Victorian Homes* magazine and founding editor of *Cottages &
Bungalows* magazine. She currently lives in Southern California
with her husband, their German shepherds, a Siamese cat, and
the occasional wandering possum. For more information, visit
www.merriedestefano.com.